The Power and Fluidity of Girlhood in Henry Darger's Art

I0474430

This book is the first to examine Henry Darger's conceptual and visual representation of "girls" and girlhood.

Specifically, Leisa Rundquist charts the artist's use of little girl imagery—his direct appropriations from mainstream sources as well as girls modified to meet his needs—in contexts that many scholars have read as puerile and psychologically disturbed. Consequently, this inquiry qualifies the intersexed aspects of Darger's protagonists as well as addresses their inherent cute and little associations that signal multivocal meanings often in conflict with each other. Rundquist engages Darger's art through thematic analyses of the artist's writings, mature works, collages, and ephemeral materials.

This book will be of particular interest to scholars in art history, art and gender studies, sociology, and contemporary art.

Leisa Rundquist is Professor of Art History in the Department of Art and Art History at the University of North Carolina Asheville, USA.

Routledge Focus on Art History and Visual Studies

For more information about this series, please visit: https://www.routledge.com/Routledge-Focus-on-Art-History-and-Visual-Studies/book-series/FOCUSAH

The Power and Fluidity of Girlhood in Henry Darger's Art

Leisa Rundquist

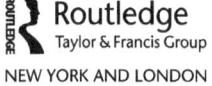

Routledge
Taylor & Francis Group

NEW YORK AND LONDON

First published 2021
by Routledge
52 Vanderbilt Avenue, New York, NY 10017

and by Routledge
2 Park Square, Milton Park, Abingdon, Oxon, OX14 4RN

Routledge is an imprint of the Taylor & Francis Group, an informa business

© 2021 Taylor & Francis

Library of Congress Cataloging-in-Publication Data
Names: Rundquist, Leisa A., author.
Title: The power and fluidity of girlhood in Henry Darger's art /
   Leisa Rundquist.
Description: New York : Routledge, 2021. | Includes
   bibliographical references and index.
Identifiers: LCCN 2020047742 (print) | LCCN 2020047743
   (ebook) | ISBN 9781138314559 (hardback) | ISBN
   9780429456886 (ebook)
Subjects: LCSH: Darger, Henry, 1892–1973—Criticism and
   interpretation. | Darger, Henry, 1892–1973—Psychology. | Girls
   in art.
Classification: LCC NX512.D37 R86 2021 (print) | LCC
   NX512.D37 (ebook) | DDC 700.92—dc23
LC record available at https://lccn.loc.gov/2020047742
LC ebook record available at https://lccn.loc.gov/2020047743

ISBN: 978-1-138-31455-9 (hbk)
ISBN: 978-0-367-74813-5 (pbk)
ISBN: 978-0-429-45688-6 (ebk)

Typeset in Times New Roman
by Apex CoVantage, LLC

Contents

Figures

Acknowledgments

Many generous and talented individuals provided feedback and support during the various stages of this book. I'd like to thank my colleagues and good friends Drs Eva Hericks Bares, Katherine Zubko, Julie Levin Caro, Ann Millett-Gallant, and Elizabeth Howie for their time and constructive criticism. Likewise, thank you to the staff at Intuit: The Center for Intuitive and Outsider Art, Chicago, for the invitation to curate "Betwixt and Between: Henry Darger's Vivian Girls" and showcase some of the developing themes in this book. Special thanks to Debra Kerr for her friendship and ongoing support. Several other individuals have been instrumental in the logistical preparation of this book. Thank you to those who assisted with securing images and rights: Alison Amick, Christina Stavos, Bob Roth, John Faier, Valérie Rousseau, Anne Marie Reilly, Vincent Monod, and the staff at Art Resource and the Artist Rights Society. Thank you to my university for making research travel possible with funding support from the UNC Asheville University Research Council and UNC Asheville Faculty Development Grant.

I would also like to acknowledge the places and organizations where I have presented papers and talks while researching and writing this book: Asheville Art Museum; Coastal Carolina University; College Art Association; Intuit; The Newberry Library Seminar in American Art; Southeastern College Art Conference; and University of North Carolina, Chapel Hill. I am grateful for those opportunities and the audiences with whom I shared my work. Finally, I thank my little family—Julia, Maggie, and Rhu—for their love and encouragement.

Introduction

He wanted the quiet rapture again. The breath of desire that arose as he had
looked over his best books. . . . The quick joy of having good times of his
babyhood days. . . . Once he had such desires but they did not return now.
They seemed to him to belong to another world . . . even if these scenes of
his younger boyhood days were given back to him, he did not believe he
would really know what to do. . . . It would be like gazing at a photograph
of a dead comrade—the days they spent together take on a mournful life in
the memory, but the boy in himself surely is no more.

—Henry Darger[1]

Like an inquisitive magpie, Henry Darger (1892–1973) stole fragments of
text and borrowed appealing images to fabricate a vibrant and tragic story.
In this passage, Darger pilfers expressions of loss and despair from Erich
Maria Ramarque's novel *All Quiet on the Western Front* (1929) revising key
phrases to shape his character's nostalgic yearning for simpler days. Just as
in this novel set within World War I, brutality and conflict equally dominate
Darger's fictional world. However, along with bloody battlefields strewn
with the dead, his art also teems with blissful children and sensuous flower
gardens. Panoramic landscapes call from afar in his compositions; their infinite horizons beckon with mystery while the capricious churning of storm
clouds signal latent danger. Little girls, embodying virtue and the mysteries
of Catholic faith, enigmatically morph and reveal male anatomy and the
resolve of warriors. Familiar pop culture imagery and narratives unravel,
shift, and gain momentum as they metamorphose into strange, contradictory
entities. Darger invites us to witness such magical transmutations, suggesting that artmaking is a recovery of childhood vision with eyes wide open. At
the heart of this adventure lie thousands upon thousands of representations
of little girls, copied and revised by the artist, seemingly possessing a primal
nature too unpredictable and protean to control completely.

The chapters that shape *The Power and Fluidity of Girlhood in Henry Darger's Art* engage aspects of his visual world through analysis of his writings, artworks, and resource materials. The frequent presence of little girls within Darger's visual art and text prompts my choice of childhood as a thematic focus and entry point into his expansive storytelling and world-building artistic practice. This book does not attempt to argue for a comprehensive, definitive interpretation of Darger's art. His imaginary world far exceeds the confines of my study. Instead, I offer a conceptual framework for approaching the art's production of meanings and by extension, contest the reduction of Darger's art to pathologic production and psycho-biographical explanation. By positioning Darger in the margins and insisting on keeping him there, scholarship fails to acknowledge that he, like other authors and artists of his time, plumbed and contributed to the rich, narrative terrain of the child. The "child," a social construction, is the product of ideas that are culturally and historically specific. Darger worked with these ideas to elicit sentimental yet provocative artworks that both support and transgress society's construction of girlhood and female agency in early to mid-twentieth-century American culture.

* * *

No one recognized Henry Darger's art until a few months before his death.[2] In December of 1972, at the age of 80, Darger was moved into a nearby convalescent facility near his home with the help of his landlords, Nathan and Kiyoko Lerner. Realizing that Darger was too infirm to return to his apartment and retrieve his belongings, Nathan Lerner initially asked Darger for his permission to clean the apartment and then began to remove forty years of clutter. In the small studio, Darger amassed heaps of eyeglass frames, Pepto-Bismol bottles, magazines, newspapers, and numerous balls of twine among other items of furniture. Lerner found a bewildering array of writings and visual art hidden beneath these oddments and collections: a 5,084-page autobiography, *The History of My Life*[3]; a ten-year journal noting Chicago's daily weather conditions and forecasts[4]; a scrapbook of newspaper clippings reporting devastating fires that Darger pasted over coloring book pages[5]; numerous, massive lexicons of pictures from popular media that Darger organized/pasted into phone books and coloring books; ledgers tabulating casualties (into the thousands) from fictional battles; loose-leaf collages he packed with human faces, hand-colored battle scenes and images of little girls and drawings of flags and military regalia. Undeniably, the most astonishing recovered items among Darger's belongings were two monumental, multi-volume texts: *The Story of the Vivian Girls, in What Is Known as the Realms of the Unreal, of the Glandeco-Angelinnian War Storm, Caused by the Child Slave Rebellion* (c. 1911–1971, hereafter, *In the*

Realms of the Unreal) of approximately 15,145 typed pages and a sequel, an untitled tale of the Vivian Girls' adventures in Chicago (started c. 1939, unfinished) of 8,000 pages. Amazed by his discovery of such unrestrained expression, Lerner approached Darger for more information about this incredible body of work, only to find reticence. "It's too late now," Darger lamented, and in a gesture of remarkable indifference, offered his apartment's contents to Lerner.[6]

Scholars estimate that Darger spent approximately twenty years writing *In the Realms of the Unreal* and nearly five decades creating artworks referencing its story. The fictional narrative of his opus describes holy wars between practitioners of child slavery—the satanic nation of Glandelinia—and the abolitionist Catholic kingdoms united under Abbieannia. In this mythic saga, the Vivian Girls, seven young Abbieannian princesses become the catalyst for insurrection and subsequent liberation of millions of indigenous, child slaves. The members of this plucky band of sisters are Violet, Joice, Jennie, Evangeline, Daisy, Hettie, and Catherine. Other main characters include their adopted sister, Gertrude Angeline; their father Robert (the emperor of Angelinia); their uncle, General Hanson Vivian; and their protector, Colonel Jack Ambrose Evans.[7] The artist even includes his own avatar, Captain Henry Darger, who is implored to participate in the war efforts due to his ability to "terrorize the enemies of children."[8] Set on an unnamed, imaginary planet, the narrative describes, with journalistic detail and cyclic repetition, battle scenes, acts of martyrdom, storms, and cataclysmic fires. Good and evil, marked by the Christian resolve of Abbieannians and murderous brutality of Glandelinians, respectively, battle throughout the multi-volumes. The conclusion of Darger's story remains unclear. Scholars note one finale celebrating the eventual triumph of the Vivians and their allies, while another storyline purports the continuance of the battle and thus, the yet-to-be-written ending. Unbound later volumes and unpaginated sections add to this ambiguity.[9]

Three bound volumes of visual artwork accompanied the written *In the Realms of the Unreal* with around 120, double-sided watercolor-drawings of various sizes—some unfolding up to twelve feet in length. Surprisingly, many watercolor-drawings reference locations and characters from the text but do not directly illustrate its story. Others appear to be non-narrative and revel in the hypnotic display of girls, flowers, and repetitive patterns. Without noting the exact number or sequence of these bound watercolor-drawings, Lerner cut each page from their hand-sewn spine and gradually introduced Darger's work as individual pictures to the art world.[10] Today, Darger's art is scattered around the globe. A complete account of its provenance and whereabouts remains unknown.[11]

He begins to write *In the Realms of the Unreal* around 1911 at the age of 19 amidst a conflated backdrop of his institutionalized and partially orphaned youth and a cultural palette expressing a modern, ever-vulnerable image of childhood.[12] Attuned to culture's child, Darger, the self-proclaimed "protector of children,"[13] clipped images of children (mostly girls) from newspapers, coloring books, and comic strips. A particular girl, Elsie Paroubek—a 5-year-old Chicagoan murdered in 1911—emerges as a fictional character in *In the Realms of the Unreal*. Frontpage newspaper coverage of Paroubek's disappearance and the subsequent discovery of her body shared prime space with commemorative articles on the American Civil War's semicentennial and the fortieth anniversary of the Great Chicago Fire. These three converging factors coincide with the inception of Darger's fictional tale of battling nation-states, child murder and enslavement, and rampant flame.

Darger went to extraordinary, arguably obsessive, efforts to tell his story in both word and image. In order to turn fiction into a war history, Darger needed accurate and available facts. He manufactured them in the form of ledgers and maps. Ledgers enumerated soldiers, providing name, rank, and casualty statistics. These numerical tallies, running up to the tens of thousands, measured the events that for Darger were ultimately enumerable in consequence.[14] Maps created a sense of place through fabrication of countries and topographies. They additionally embodied a form of imaginary travel, offering opportunities for the artist and viewer to re-trace journeys and the progress of invading armies. To further establish accuracy, Darger created an extensive visual archive by assembling files and scrapbooks of clipped newspaper articles and photographs, daily comic strips and comic books, coloring books, magazine illustrations, and fashion advertisements. These sources provided documentary and fantastic images of fires, explosions, cloud formations, soldiers, flora and fauna, architecture, and little girls. Along with this source material, Darger's visual lexicon grew from compiling addenda on warfare and imperialistic regalia—hundreds of drawings/collages of flags, soldiers' uniforms, and weaponry—appropriated from popular culture sources and amended by his hand. Newspaper coverage of World War I and II, as well as reports on the Spanish Civil War and commemorative pieces on the American Civil War provided rich sources for historicized militaristic adornment and armaments. While some resource material is fully colored and naturalistic, Darger oriented his collecting efforts toward graphic and stylized black and white imagery that could be easily transferred into his fictional world. Tracing became Darger's essential tool for artmaking. This method of drawing coupled with an extensive trove of stock images allowed for a seemingly inexhaustible amount of recursive and reworked material to fill his paintings.

Photographs and engravings supplied the material for Darger's early collage works prior to 1932. Predominately devoid of children, these hand-colored images featured appropriated photographs of soldiers and battle scenes from newspapers and magazines. After this date he transitioned into tracing to produce images. With so much visual and narrative information to offer, Darger turned toward two predominate visual modes to articulate his opus: expansive panoramic landscapes and the sequential narrative of comic strip frames. Panoramic formats serve as a popular visual standard in American culture for illustrating battles, ruins, and majestic landscapes. The various battle scenes that Darger clipped from magazines and incorporated into his own artwork demonstrate his familiarity with this convention. By the same token, comic strips from the early twentieth century offered short and direct progressive narratives complete with image and text. Some of Darger's favorites that he archived include stories about girl orphan *Little Annie Rooney* (1927–1966) and master of hypnosis *Mandrake the Magician* (1934–2013). Two single and double-paneled comics that Darger fanatically collected, *There Oughta Be a Law* (1944–1985) and *They'll Do It Every Time* (1929–2008) humorously speak to the hypocrisies and ironies of daily life. Each of these formats supports multiple, complex changes regarding figures within their environments that infer a slow animation of bodies and weather phenomena informing Darger's representations.

He continued to compile many scrapbooks and files into the 1950s and 1960s—near the latter part of his life and creative output. Files, scrapbooks, and ledgers appear to follow a central purpose to compliment and complete his written epic. Although presenting a fictitious history, Darger's written introduction for the second volume assures his reader (and himself) that all "facts" for his fictional tale are solid and have proper documentation.

The stories in this volume have been reproduced after most careful patient work and from original battles known in other sections of the great and intolerable war.

All the incidents in this volume are fully intended to give the reader and the others, in the best way as possible a complete and most accurate account of this great conflict as far as the volume goes, describing in entertaining language some more of the strange and sad circumstances that led to the record breaking struggle, the most important battles of that time on land and water, the kind of soldiers on both sides who so fiercely and insanely participated in them and the causes that brought such shameful disasters and downfalls of some of the national armies.

The description with the interesting written illustrations will, it is hoped, bring about a far better knowledge and more correct idea of the fierce and sanguinary progress of the Abbieannian Intercine war than volume One first presented to the public.

Neither trouble nor expense has been spared to make this volume perfectly reliable in every way. Editors of great experience will be in due time allowed to go over the whole work most carefully and verify every date of incidents, disasters, battles and great adventures so as to prevent the possibility of error.[15]

Darger's pride in his archival work comes through in this address to the reader. Even experienced editors will corroborate the story's faithful adherence to data. His concern for accuracy also echoes his school-boy frustrations over the inconsistencies in Civil War histories. In *The History of My Life* (1967–1970) he writes,

> I once told my teacher, but the one, Mrs. Dewey at the Skinner school, that I believed no one truthfully knew the losses in the battles of wars (including our Civil War), because each history told different losses, and I had the histories and other stories to prove it.[16]

Darger's love of reading and retention of facts equaled that of his "entertaining language," or penchant for hyperbole. Both may well have been fed by Chicago journalism and its reporting of horrific accounts from World War I and later, World War II, as well as lurid stories of child abductions and murders noted later in this book.

Darger also had an eye for sentiments capturing the sweetness and vulnerability of childhood. Loosely basing his story upon the horrors of slavery and the disruption of familial ties during the American Antebellum period and Civil War, Darger appropriates whole paragraphs from Harriet Beecher Stowe's *Uncle Tom's Cabin* (1852), and especially, the character of Stowe's angelic protagonist, Little Eva.[17] Likewise, fantasy worlds and wonder tales influenced his prose as he incorporated places and characters from L. Frank Baum's *Oz* series (1900–1920) and perhaps appropriated the word "unreal" for his own title from Baum's preface to *The Wonderful Wizard of Oz* (1900): "Folk lore, legends, myths, and fairy tales have followed childhood through the ages, for every healthy youngster has a wholesome and instinctive love for stories fantastic, marvelous, and manifestly unreal."[18] However whimsical and naive his creation appeared on the surface, Darger did realize its difference from the fairy tale of Oz. In his story, he wonders how the characters of Oz would fare in his dangerous Realms of the Unreal:

> I have read many of the beautiful Oz books, and have read that in that kind of country no one, whether man, woman, or children, or beasts, ever become sick or die . . . what would the people of Oz do if their country had been somewhere in Calverinia unknown to the Calverinians, and Glinda would see in her great record book, "Great

Glandelinian army advancing on the Emerald City. Rebel army pursuing Angelinians. Glandelinian army one hundred million strong."[19]

In a later unbound volume, Darger warns, "This is not the land of Oz where Dorothy and her Oz friends reside."[20] At a cursory glance, Darger's art appears to be a children's story drenched in exuberant color and patterns with action-packed scenes inhabited by toy soldiers and girls from coloring books and comics. Deeper within, unabashed violence, murder, and misogynistic abuse abounds. Through the lens of his girl protagonists, Darger fabricated a world where childhood innocence and safety were continuously in peril. Along with soldiers, child slaves died in the thousands. Many experienced tortured, painful deaths. Darger's *In the Realms of the Unreal* pivots back and forth on this teetering axis of childhood saved and childhood lost. In contrast, his own childhood was far less sensational and fantastic but still deeply affected by familial loss, impoverished circumstances, and institutional privation.

Childhood

Henry Darger grew up in Chicago, a few decades after the Great Fire of 1871, during a tumultuous era framed by tremendous growth, political unrest, and growing concerns for child welfare. The nation's second largest urban center gloated over the dignified presence of its neoclassical "White City,"[21] while aldermen prospered financially in the vice and trafficking of prostitution in the Levee District.[22] British journalist William T. Stead condemned Chicago in 1894 as "a cyclone of moral indignation," pointing out the irony of hungry masses in a city with abundant supplies of grain and stockyards.[23] The Progressive Era (1870–1930) ushered children's rights to the fore as reforms in medicine, insurance, and child labor evolved into civic concerns for the physical welfare of the child. With issues such as the "moral hazards of the streets,"—the estimation of 5,000 children daily in busy Chicago thoroughfares (boot-blacks, "newsies," delivery boys, and myriad numbers of vagrants)—growing streams of spiritual, sentimental, and government reforms elevated the sacralization of children's lives to public policy.[24] Sociologist Viviana Zelizer refers to this era's phenomenon of the "priceless child," arguing that American society shifted from valuing children less in economic terms and more in sentimental and emotional ones. Along with the growing taboo of child labor, Zelizer also cites civic concerns for child mortality rates: "child death became an intolerable sacrilege, provoking not only parental sorrow but social bereavement as well."[25] A child's death, regardless of his/her social class, exceeded a sense of "a painful domestic misfortune" and rose to the level of "collective failure."[26]

Furthermore, the murder of a child "emerged as a singularly obnoxious and almost sacrilegious crime."[27] As chapters in this book contend, Darger fully absorbed these attitudes concerning this novel, sentimental valuation of children. Evident in the inflated child worship in his art, he also discloses a personal devotion to the well-being of children in his autobiography:

> You remember I wrote that I hated baby kids. So indeed I did. Yet what a change came in me though when I grew somewhat older. These babies at that were more to me than anything, more than the world. I would fondle them and love them. At that time just any bigger boy or even grown up dare molest or harm them in any way.[28]

In spite of this passage, other nuances of Henry Darger's private life and childhood as well as his feelings regarding the adversities of his upbringing are relatively unknown. What we do understand about Darger centers around a trajectory of his misfortunes. These hardships begin when he was four when his mother died during childbirth. Darger's father immediately gave up the newborn sister for adoption. At age 8, Darger experienced the loss of his father's presence in his life, shortly after he was sent to The Mission of Our Lady of Mercy boys' home. Bouncing around from parochial schools, to Catholic boys' homes, and, at age 13, entering the Lincoln Asylum for Feeble-Minded Children for "self-abuse," a euphemism for masturbation, Darger lived most of his adolescent years in institutions.[29] His lack of social skills and non-conformative behavior tested the resolve of many educators, clergy, and physicians.[30] Beginning around age 16, after hearing of his father's death, Darger attempted three escapes from the asylum. On the third attempt in 1909, he succeeded and walked back to Chicago from central Illinois. He lived the remainder of his life quietly, working in Catholic-run hospitals as a janitor, dishwasher, and in his late years, as general help in kitchens and stock rooms. Attending Catholic Mass daily, sometimes thrice, Darger jokes in his autobiography of being a "sorry saint."[31]

Despite unremitting poverty and the difficulties in Henry Darger's life, *The History of My Life* (1968–1972) rarely reflects upon his struggles. Or, better said, his journaling lacks the same kind of vigor and loquaciousness that one finds in the telling of his fictional story. Cultural critic Olivia Laing astutely describes Darger's autobiography as a "narrative of gaps."[32] She notes the benign nature of his account of childhood, including Darger's description of the feeble-minded asylum, an institution notorious for its abuse of inmates[33] as "sometimes was pleasant and sometimes not so."[34] Consequently, she attributes his terse remarks and absences of detail as a sign of Darger's isolation and acquiescence to decades of socio-economic powerlessness. The lack of detail in his autobiography coupled by its de-evolution into a fictional tale of a tornado named, "Sweetie Pie" has led many scholars to fill in those gaps. While we don't know if Darger was abused mentally, physically, or sexually at this asylum or other facilities, some scholars note that probability, while others make outright assumptions based upon the violence and disturbing erotics of Darger's imagery.[35] Likewise in his autobiography, Darger appears reticent to elaborate on *In the Realms of the Unreal* or related artworks that he spent decades on. Instead, remarks about creating artwork surface indirectly, as in this example complaining about his aches and pains: "To make matters worse now I'm an artist, been one for years and cannot hardly stand on my feet because of my knee to paint on the top of the long picture."[36] Overall, Darger offers little to no insight into the major experiences of his life and impairments that one would expect to read in an autobiography.

Darger never married or had children but he did express a wish to adopt an orphaned child. In an unconventional plea, he makes that goal apparent in a series of posed questions on two typed petitions in 1929 and 1930 pertaining to an anonymous "desirous man" wanting to adopt children.[37] Strangely marked with a handwritten notation, "found on sidewalk," these questions are interpreted by art historian John M. MacGregor to be a manifestation of Darger's internalized struggles with his faith. In this segment, Darger reveals his frustration:

> As it is really true that God knows a person's farthest future, is it the facts of the person's responsibilities in the case of adopting a child, that keeps the favor from being answered, or is it just God's way to try his faith and also his patience?[38]

Whether or not Darger formally petitioned his local Catholic Church to adopt a child is not known. The questions and relating commentary, however, indicate that Darger was given some feedback, perhaps from a priest, and that he agonized over God's and the Church's lack of support for twelve years.

Bringing together sparse biographical details as well as a wealth of ephemeral sources belonging to Darger, specific interests and behaviors come to the forefront when examining his life. The two that emphatically stand out are his attunement to cultural constructions of the vulnerability and virtue of children and the significance of his Catholic faith. Both play substantial roles in the storyline of *In the Realms of the Unreal*, comprise large sections of his resource collections and personal library, figure prominently in his autobiography, and remain visible in his home environment. Religious practices equally presented in his daily life. Accounts of attending Mass, often more than once a day, walking through the Stations of the

Cross, confession, and attending novenas and Holy Communion fill *The History of my Life.*

Certainly, Darger's religious practices gave structure to his day-to-day experiences. They are a constant and stable component of his childhood and adult existence even when he questions his faith.

Previous Scholarship

Initial scholarship of Darger's visual work interprets it in two frames: first, a Freudian analysis disclosing the trauma of the artist's childhood and second, a paradigm of outsider art (a construct selectively incorporating frame one). John M. MacGregor's *Henry Darger: In the Realms of the Unreal* (2002) presented the first critical discussion.[39] In addition to composing an important biographical sketch of Darger's formative years, MacGregor (a psychotherapist, art historian, and author of *Discovery of the Art of the Insane* (1989)) offers psychoanalytic interpretations on specific elements of Darger's life and work. Overall, MacGregor argues that Darger's art symbolizes a "depiction of an internal mental state: a deeply troubled and troubling externalization of traumatic experiences distressingly familiar to Henry Darger; a revisiting of scenes from his own childhood."[40] MacGregor begins, "Henry Darger is most commonly, and correctly, classified as an 'Outsider artist.' In Europe, his work has found acceptance as 'Art Brut.' . . . (these artists) are not generally interested in 'making art.'"[41] MacGregor provides a list of other activities and outcomes that he attributes to the creative production of the outsider artist. Some examples include: "making maps to orient themselves within the experience of insanity," "representing their personal visions of God," and "embodying strange delusions about sex, politics, or religion."[42] Overall, MacGregor argues that the goal of the outsider artist is to create an alternative world that alters a lived reality. In this monograph, as in other accounts, an interpretive framework for Darger's art emerges as points of difference from accepted norms of mainstream society and art. MacGregor sums up his introductory statements by reasserting that this study of Henry Darger,

> An important Outsider artist will help to clarify the nature of this unusual form of (outsider) art, identifying the essential characteristics which mark it off as a form of expression distinct from, and yet surprisingly relevant to, all other forms of contemporary art.[43]

This statement from the introduction of his study on Henry Darger explicitly suggests that MacGregor undertook his research with a conclusion already in mind. He prematurely classifies and simplifies Darger's work, rendering it rudimentary by modeling it into an example of outsider art.

Subsequent interpretations of Darger's art follow MacGregor's lead, labeling Darger as the art world's consummate "outsider artist"—an individual free of exterior, cultural influences and the contaminating effects of the art world. British art historian Roger Cardinal coined the term "outsider art" in his eponymous 1972 publication, heralding the anti-cultural sentiments of artist/collector, Jean Dubuffet (1901–1985). Outsider art, Cardinal's term, introduces French *art brut*, Dubuffet's 1945 discovery, to an English-speaking audience. Within this text, Cardinal extends and re-defines Dubuffet's *brut*, or "raw" art, beyond the context of asylum artistry: "not only the art of the clinically insane, but also other art of an authentically untutored, original and extra-cultural nature."[44] The following appears in *Outsider Art* as Dubuffet's standard *art brut* definition:

> We understand by this term works produced by persons unscathed by artistic culture, where mimicry plays little or no part (contrary to the activities of intellectuals). These artists derive everything—subjects, choice of materials, means of transposition, rhythms, styles of writing, etc.—from their own depths, and not from the conventions of classical or fashionable art. We are witness here to a completely pure artistic operation, raw, brute, and entirely reinvented in all of its phases solely by means of the artists' own impulses. It is thus an art which manifests an unparalleled inventiveness, unlike cultural art, with its chameleon— and monkey—like aspects.[45]

Dubuffet's description of *art brut*, applied by Cardinal as the precedent of outsider art, implies that western culture pollutes the very essence of art, sullying it with its inherent derivations. Likewise, intellectuals operate in a monkey-like fashion, oblivious to their own mimicry. *Brut* artists, on the other hand, follow their own instincts, upholding a sacred and natural purity in their creations. The *art brut* artist and the intellectual represent a polarity of Nature (self) and Culture (society), respectively.

Quotes defining *art brut* proliferate throughout Cardinal's text. Oddly enough, the nomenclature "outsider art" only appears on the cover of Cardinal's publication. As "outsider" is never directly defined or remarked upon in the book's body, it appears that the title came after the text, and that Cardinal opted for the term not as a translation, but as a synonymic, perhaps more marketable variation. *Brut*, in its various English translations, runs a gamut of meanings from *clownish* to *pure*.[46] It is plausible that Cardinal and his editors found the translation of *brut* to be problematic, and "outsider," made popular by Colin Wilson's *The Outsider* (1956, 1967 editions) seemed more palatable and familiar for an English-speaking audience. Wilson's critically acclaimed sociological study argues for the necessity of "outsiders" in western culture and provides a model for imagining them through well-known works of literature and visual art by Ernest Hemingway, Fyodor Dostoevsky, and Vincent Van Gogh, among many others. According to Wilson, the outsider is the mainstay of the bourgeois, providing vitality and "soul-energy."[47] The outsider's course of expression is determined by intensity, extremes of experience, and detachment from society. Romanticized by mainstream culture, the outsider's world appears "tragically, impossibly distant" from average life.[48] Similarly, Cardinal's outsider artist operates in his or her own art-making world, self-taught in technique, creating without the limitations and boundaries often affecting and suppressing trained artists, such as capitalism, social mores, and in some instances, psychological repression. As such, Cardinal posits that the isolate outsider creates a naturally instinctive, authentic, original, and thus, revolutionary art.

Cardinal's benchmark for outsider creativity, what MacGregor later bases Darger's status on, is self-imposed isolation, estrangement or alienation—a notion that problematically collapses social and artistic non-conformity. In this outsider model, one is lead to believe that Darger's disenfranchised status and supposed psychological disturbances heighten his artistic value. He is celebrated as an aesthetic rebel who contests cultural norms and artistic traditions. Accordingly, MacGregor insinuates that Darger's intense artistic practice is a "rejection of reality . . . reflective of a massively abnormal, though not necessarily pathological, state of consciousness."[49]

Much scholarship on Henry Darger's art involves this outsider label without question, claiming outsider status as the foundation of research even though it offers little more than extra-canonical positioning. One often encounters highly subjective pronouncements of Darger's history of physical and sexual abuse, even pedophilic tendencies, among other differences from "normality" as part of his self-evident outsider determination and a priori formulas.[50] Such emphasis on Darger's outsider artist status illustrates sociologist Eugene Metcalf, Jr.'s claim that, "the discourse on Outsider Art does not really think about, observe, or critically study the outsider. It thinks, observes, and studies in *terms* of the outsider."[51] Consequently, categorical models placed upon Henry Darger fail to acknowledge his engagement with American culture and deny him a sense of agency.

The 2002 study by MacGregor remains the authoritative text on Darger's art; however, scholarly interests in relying on psycho-biographical methods have waned in recent years in favor of research that considers cultural influences in tandem with the artist's material resources. My approach to the art of Henry Darger aligns with and expands upon this research, specifically that of Michael Bonesteel, a specialist in outsider art; Michael Moon, literary critic; and Mary Trent, art historian. Bonesteel's focus on Darger's writings uncovers multiple appropriated sources and speaks to the author's working methods.[52] Exercising cultural frameworks, Moon reveals how the dark recesses of proletarian print culture shed light on Darger's gory and elegiac art. Doing so, his scholarship locates intersections between sexuality, class, and religion in his art and writings.[53] And finally, Trent's inquiry into Darger's collage processes exposes how the artist addresses topical concerns for child safety and social anxiety aimed at deviancy and sexual predators.[54]

The chapters that shape *The Power and Fluidity of Girlhood in Henry Darger's Art* broaden this recent scholarship through inclusive and interdisciplinary modes and by reading Darger's artistic production as a personal mythology filtering and re-interpreting culture. This book is the first to examine Henry Darger's conceptual and visual representation of "girls" and girlhood. Specifically, I chart the artist's use of little girl imagery—his direct appropriations from mainstream sources as well as girls modified to meet his needs—in contexts that many scholars have read as puerile and psychologically disturbed. Consequently, my inquiry qualifies the intersexed aspects of Darger's protagonists as well as addresses their inherent cute and little associations that signal multivocal meanings often in conflict with each other. As a result, the following chapters test the simple façade of the little girl image and thus, reveal the power dynamics and fluid range of interpretations that she engenders in Darger's art.

Chapter 1, "Littleness" begins to unpack the cultural connotations informing the diminutive state of Darger's "little" girls and their resource material. Exploring this material (comic strip, advertising, and coloring book imagery), I argue that Darger appropriates not only the visible attributes of girlhood but also its visual constructs. In this chapter, I contend that Darger fabricates a particular notion of littleness—a blend of romantic Victorian childhood, girl saints, and floral Marian tropes—from such popular characters referenced by Darger in his art and writings: Shirley Temple's "The Littlest Rebel," "Little Eva" of *Uncle Tom's Cabin*, and Saint Thérèse of Lisieux, also known as "The Little Flower of Christ." Purity and innocence surface in the first two exemplars of girlhood while virtue and self-sacrificing qualities link to the girlish nature and humble floral metaphors of Saint Thérèse. Additionally, this chapter explores the etymology of the name, "Vivian," and contextualizes it within the vitality of Darger's Vivian Girls and their instinctual knack for survival.

Chapter 2, "Girls on the Run," scrutinizes the representation of girls with intersex characteristics. My reading of Darger's girls embraces the term "intersex" as it encompasses broad biological variation and differences in "sex traits or reproductive anatomy."[55] "Intersex," is the most suitable way to describe Darger's rendition of girls due to their non-binary ambiguity. I refer to the Vivians as "girls," as that is the artist's description used throughout his story and imagery even when his representations blur anatomical boundaries. Darger's art appears to embrace a spectrum of gender and sex even though he gleaned his imagery from conventional gender/sex-conforming resources that reinstate mainstream society's representations of girlhood. Vast amounts of ephemera collected and traced by the artist of little girl fashions signal that Darger was keenly aware of society's determination of girlish femininity and its commercial trappings. He replicated the petticoats, braided ponytails, and Mary Jane shoes comprising attire for girls ages 7–12 and dressed the denizens of the *In the Realms of the Unreal* in the codes and conventions of the day that outwardly announced their age-appropriate femininity. However, the Vivians and their girl counterparts contradict binary associations conferred by their attire. Partially dressed and nude bodies reveal a playful fluidity that defies standard categorizations of sex. These girls, mostly in motion, display penciled-in schematic male genitalia—a puzzling component of Darger's art that he does not explain.

Consequently, while acknowledging the frequency and thus significance of girl crusaders with intersex characteristics, this chapter posits relationships between Darger's Vivian Girls and female saints celebrated in Catholic devotional cults. His appropriation and use of holy cards, martyr narratives, as well as his own variations on specific martyrs' names and their legendary ambiguous gender suggest a divine lineage between the Vivians and female martyrs like SS. Vivia Perpetua and Joan of Arc. Within Darger's invocation of sacred childhood lies Catholic religiosity and stories of gender-bending female saints who inform Darger's conception of holy, brave, and transgressive girlhood. Pursuing these connections, this chapter opens the possibilities for further discussion of Darger's Vivians within broad-ranging, less sexually fetishized frameworks by bringing the image of these extraordinary children into the context of art and religion.

Chapter 3, "The Power of Cuteness," decodes the visual aesthetics of cuteness and its language of commodified childhood that are intrinsically embedded in Darger's art. His legions of child warriors, led by the Vivian Girls, embody a historically and culturally specific notion of aesthetic perfection and thus participate in a wider cultural production and consumption of a particular, racialized and idealized type of girl. My scholarship contends that child star, Shirley Temple sets a precedent and crucial example for Darger's imagined child. Drawing from film studies, literary criticism, and studies in the aesthetic of cuteness, this chapter speaks to the ways in which Darger alerts us to cuteness's proximity to both adoration and violence. Appropriated from a commodified and thus already desirous gaze, cute characters in his art invite affectionate involvement and congenial feelings. They also become a site for both establishing and testing the polarities of goodness and cruelty, vulnerability and power, as well as innocence and sexuality. I close with an epilogue that analyzes how Darger establishes relationships between panoramic formats and the attentive gazes of little girl multitudes that acknowledge and imply the viewer's presence in his art. Internally within paintings these girls do not visually correspond; their attentiveness to the viewer creates an implied sense of cohesion resulting not from formal composition but instead from this performative act. This attentive action dovetails with Darger's written appeal to a "Dear Reader" in his introductions. Both devices, one aesthetic and the other rhetorical, attempt to fully immerse his audience (even if imagined) and to witness events in *In the Realms of the Unreal*. Ultimately, this book illustrates how Darger's representations of little girls elicit disparate meanings simultaneously within different contexts. In his creation of the fictional Vivian Girl, Darger brings into focus three discourses—public concerns regarding the sanctity of childhood during the early to mid-twentieth century, his own intimate imaginings of the girl as a site of limitless potential, and current day attitudes regarding innocence and sexuality that still inform conceptions of girlhood.

Notes

1 Henry Darger, *The Story of the Vivian Girls, in What is Known as the Realms of the Unreal, of the Glandeco-Angelinnian War Storm, Caused by the Child Slave Rebellion* (unpublished, c. 1911–1939, microfilm, Henry Darger Papers) (New York: American Folk Art Museum Library and Archives) as quoted in the documentary, *In the Realms of the Unreal: The Mystery of Henry Darger*, Director Jessica Yu, Diorama Films, 2005. Hereafter in the footnotes, Darger's story will be abbreviated to *In the Realms on the Unreal* to correlate with the common abbreviation used throughout current scholarship and in the body of this chapter. Darger's words are revisions from *All Quite on the Western Front* (1929) by Erich Maria Remarque: "I want that quiet rapture again. I want to feel the same powerful, nameless urge that I used to feel when I turned to my books. The breath of desire that then arose from the coloured backs of the books, shall fill me again, melt the heavy, dead lump of lead that lies somewhere in me and waken again the impatience of the future, the quick joy in the world of thought, it shall bring back again the lost eagerness of my youth." "Once we had such desires—but they return not. They are past, they belong to another world that is gone from us." ". . . would be like gazing at the photograph of a dead comrade; those are his features, it is his face, and the days we spent together take on a mournful life in memory; but the man himself it is not." Erich Maria Remarque, *All Quiet on the Western Front*, trans. A. W. Wheen (Boston, MA: Little, Brown & Company, 1986 [1929]), 173, 121, 122.

2 According to landlord Kiyoko Lerner and neighbor David Berglund, each saw either a piece of Darger's art in his apartment or witnessed him making it. Darger's isolation appears to have been a two-way relationship; no one took

much interest in Darger's activities and Darger kept his artmaking to himself. Michael Bonesteel writes, "Kiyoko recalled going into his room on one occasion to change a light bulb and noticing a drawing on the table." "Henry, you're a good artist," she remarked. "Yes," replied Darger. "I am." Bonesteel continues, "Berglund also remembered going into Darger's room one day and seeing him work." "I looked over his shoulder as he was doing one of his big paintings. He was very happy doing this, singing a song quietly to himself." Michael Bonesteel, *Henry Darger: Art and Selected Writings* (New York: Rizzoli Press, 2000), 13.

3 *The History of My Life* contains two separate stories, the first is an autobiographical narrative up to page 206 followed by the second, what Darger called, "A Fictional Story of a Huge Twister Called 'Sweetie Pie.'" Henry Darger, *The History of My Life* (unpublished, 1967–1970, microfilm, Henry Darger Papers) (New York: American Folk Art Museum Library and Archives).

4 Notations in the weather books begin on January 1, 1958 (when Darger was 65 years old) and continue through December 31, 1967. Henry Darger, *Weather Report of Cold and Warm, Also Summer Heats and Cool Spells, Storms and Fair or Cloudy Days Contrary to What the Weatherman Says, and Also True Too* (unpublished, 1958–1967, microfilm, Henry Darger Papers) (New York: American Folk Art Museum Library and Archives).

5 This scrapbook, *Pictures of Fires Big or Small in Which Firemen or Persons Lose Their Lives*, recorded deadly fires from Chicago and other urban centers dating from the 1950s to 1960s. Darger also used this scrapbook to augment his collection of fire and storm pictures. Graphite marks along the outlines of smoke and cloud formations reveal that he studied and appropriated the articles' photographic imagery. Henry Darger, *Pictures of Fires Big or Small in Which Firemen or Persons Lose Their Lives* (unpublished, c. 1950–1960, Henry Darger Room Collection and Archives) (Chicago: Intuit: The Center for Intuitive and Outsider Art).

6 Considering that Darger was probably aware of his approaching death, being "too late" in regards to his art may suggest his inextricable connection to the life and vitality of his projects. Darger's neighbor, David Berglund recounts, "I visited him in the home, just once. I looked at him and said, 'Henry, you have paintings in the room!' He got this look in his eyes . . . it wasn't just the look, it was like I'd taken the wind out of him, and his eyes kind of moistened, and he said, 'It's too late now,' and he didn't want to talk about it." John M. MacGregor, *Henry Darger: In the Realms of the Unreal* (New York: Delano Greenidge Editions, 2002), 84.

7 For a thorough account of characters in Darger's *In the Realms of the Unreal* see Michael Bonesteel, "Henry Darger's Search for the Holy Grail in the Guise of a Celestial Child," in *Third Person: Authoring and Exploring Vast Narratives*, edited by Pat Harrigan and Noah Wardrip-Fruin (Cambridge: MIT Press, 2009), 253.

8 Captain Darger is asked for his help in a letter penned by Colonel Jack Evans: "From two friends of mine I have learned of your ability of terrorizing the enemies of children. You of course must have heard of the great child slave trades going on in Calverinia." Darger, *In the Realms of the Unreal*, Volume I, 61 as quoted in MacGregor, *In the Realms of the Unreal*, 96.

9 See MacGregor, *In the Realms of the Unreal*, 115 and Bonesteel, "Henry Darger's Search for the Holy Grail," 264.

10 Nathan Lerner retrieved three volumes of illustrations from Darger's apartment. In 1977, Lerner organized the first exhibition of Darger's work at Chicago's Hyde Park Art Center.

11 Twenty visual works (double-sided), along with numerous, smaller collages, Darger's writings, and his collection of literature and ephemera, comprise the Henry Darger Papers at New York's American Folk Art Museum Library and Archives. Intuit: The Center for Intuitive and Outsider Art, Chicago, owns Darger's personal effects, artmaking materials, some newspaper clippings, and numerous scrapbooks, including *Pictures of Fires Big and Small* as part of the Henry Darger Room Collection and Archives.

12 Bonesteel approximates that Darger began writing in long-hand between 1910 and 1912. He switched to typing his manuscript in 1916 and began hand-binding his volumes in 1932. His final seven or eight volumes remained unbound and thus, the ending of Darger's story shows no obvious, final conclusion. Bonesteel, "Henry Darger's Search for the Holy Grail," 25.

13 MacGregor, *In the Realms of the Unreal*, 62. In addition to this title, Darger describes a fictional children's protection society known as the "Gemini" in *In the Realms of the Unreal* which he and his friend, Whilliam Schloeder oversee.

14 MacGregor estimates that Darger's listing of soldiers runs into the tens of thousands. MacGregor, *In the Realms of the Unreal*, 107.

15 Darger, *In the Realms of the Unreal*, Volume II, Introduction (unpaginated).

16 Darger, *History of My Life*, 19–20.

17 Darger's reach extended well beyond the texts mentioned in my Introduction. According to Bonesteel, Darger borrowed from Catholic prayers, Henry Wadsworth Longfellow, and Jules Verne, among many others. See Bonesteel, "Henry Darger's Search for the Holy Grail," 255, 257–260.

18 L. Frank Baum, *The Wonderful Wizard of Oz* (New York: HarperCollins Publishers, 1900 [1987]), 5.

19 Darger, *In the Realms of the Unreal*, Volume VII, 233.

20 Quoted in MacGregor, *In the Realms of the Unreal*, 99 from Darger, *In the Realms of the Unreal*, Volume XII, unbound 12–13.

21 The "white city" became the moniker of plastered, neoclassical white-washed buildings at the 1893 World Columbian Exposition. See James R. Grossman, ed., "World's Columbian Exposition," in *The Encyclopedia of Chicago* (Chicago: The University of Chicago Press, 2004), 899.

22 According to Chicago lore, the phrase "red light district" stems from the ubiquitous red glass used in transoms of the notorious Levee District's brothels. Prostitution in Chicago was a multi-million-dollar business and politicians provided protection from police raids. See Lisa Krissoff Boehm, *Popular Culture and the Enduring Myth of Chicago, 1876–1968* (Philadelphia: Routledge, 2004), 84.

23 Stead was particularly aghast at the 3,000 men who were fed daily by the city's saloons (far outnumbering those receiving aid from charitable social or church organizations). During election time, these men returned the favor with votes. William T. Stead, *If Christ Came to Chicago!* (Chicago: Laird & Lee, 1894), 244 and 268.

24 For a history of the social ramifications of the United States' Progressive Era and child-saving crusades, see Viviana A. Zelizer, *Pricing the Priceless Child: The Changing Social Value of Children* (New York: Basic Books, 1985).

25 Zelizer, *Pricing the Priceless Child*, 23.

26 Ibid, 32.

27 Ibid, 49.
28 Darger, *History of My Life*, 9.
29 MacGregor recounts the application that Darger's father and a physician completed for his son's clinical assessment. Among several questions, the men answered "self-abuse" as an indicator of mental deficiency. MacGregor, *In the Realms of the Unreal*, 45.
30 Darger often remarked about his indulgent and difficult behavior in his *History of My Life*: "From the time I was a young boy, until even now, I always had a very rough nature or temper, always was and still am self-willed and also determined that at all costs, even at the expense of Sin, that all things shall come my way, no matter what might try to interfere or stand in my way." Michael Bonesteel, *Henry Darger: Art and Selected Writings* (New York: Rizzoli, 2000), 8.
31 "I go to three morning Masses and communion every day, and one extra Mass on Sunday afternoon. And on Mondays, I go to the Miraculous Medal Novena Devotion. It too is followed by Mass. What did you say? I am a saint? Ha, ha. I am one, and a very sorry saint I am. Ha, ha. How can I be a saint when I won't stand for trials, bad luck, pains in my knees or otherwise." Darger, *History of My Life* as quoted by Bonesteel, *Henry Darger*, 31.
32 Olivia Laing, "The Realms of the Unreal," in *Lonely City: Adventures in the Art of Being Alone* (New York: Picador, 2016), 142.
33 MacGregor notes several instances of abuse in his study on Darger. MacGregor, *In the Realms of the Unreal*, 536–537. Bonesteel notes the asylum's reputation in "Henry Darger's Search for the Grail," 254.
34 Darger, *History of My Life* as quoted by Laing, "The Realms of the Unreal," 144.
35 See Chapter 3 for further comments by scholar John M. MacGregor.
36 Darger, *History of My Life*, 163.
37 MacGregor cites these questions as evidence of Darger's desire to adopt. He also notes a handwritten address for the Dependent Child Commission in Chicago, which Darger may have also contacted. See MacGregor, *In the Realms of the Unreal*, 638–641.
38 Quoted in MacGregor, *In the Realms of the Unreal*, 639.
39 Primary literature on Darger and his art include: MacGregor's *In the Realms of the Unreal*. Bonesteel's *Henry Darger* precedes MacGregor's text and offers an overview of Darger's art and life based upon MacGregor's unpublished notes and a catalogue written by MacGregor for the Collection de *l'art brut*, *Henry J. Darger: Dans les Royaumes de 'llrréel* (Lausanne: Fondazione Galleria Gottardo, 1990). The American Museum of Folk Art published a catalogue, *Darger: The Henry Darger Collection at the American Folk Art Museum*, ed. Brooke Davis Anderson (New York: Harry N. Abrams, 2001) with a short essay by Michel Thévoz, former director of the *art brut* collection in Lausanne, Switzerland.
40 MacGregor, *In the Realms of the Unreal*, 21.
41 Ibid.
42 Ibid, 20.
43 Ibid, 21.
44 Although Dubuffet collected works from inmates inside and individuals outside asylums, his theoretical stance on anti-cultural purity privileged the social and psychological circumstances of asylum art. As a result, *art brut* is often incorrectly translated as "Art of the Insane." For cited quote, see Roger Cardinal, *Outsider Art* (New York: Praeger Publishers, 1972), 24.

45 Jean Dubuffet, "Art Brut in Preference to the Cultural Arts," trans. Paul Foss and Allen S. Weiss, *Art & Text* 27 (1998): 33. Dubuffet's essay originally appeared in the *Art Brut* catalogue at the Galerie René Drouin in Paris, October 1949.

46 Colin Rhodes believes that Dubuffet chose the term *brut* because of its resistance to a precise definition. See Colin Rhodes, *Outsider Art: Spontaneous Alternatives* (New York: Thames and Hudson, 2000), 23.

47 Colin Wilson, *The Outsider* (New York: Penguin Putnam, 1982, 1967, 1956), 59.

48 Ibid, 234. Wilson's critically acclaimed, *The Outsider* (1956, revised 1967) preceded Cardinal's 1972 publication.

49 MacGregor, *In the Realms of the Unreal*, 21.

50 Some examples include Daniel Wojcik's statements that, "In the asylum, Darger experienced brutal physical abuse" and "other critics find evidence in his work that he was a potential mass murder, with possible pedophilic tendencies, and that the sublimation of these urges through art kept him from acting out violent impulses." Daniel Wojcik, *Outsider Art: Visionary Worlds and Trauma* (Jackson, MS: University Press of Mississippi, 2016), 65, 67.

51 Eugene W. Metcalf Jr., "From Domination to Desire: Insiders and Outsider Art," in *The Artist Outsider: Creativity and the Boundaries of Culture*, edited by Eugene W. Metcalf Jr. and Michael D. Hall (Washington, DC: Smithsonian Institution Press, 1994), 220.

52 See Bonesteel, *Henry Darger* and "Henry Darger's Search for the Grail."

53 Michael Moon, *Darger's Resources* (Durham: Duke University Press, 2012).

54 Mary Trent, "Enigmatic Bachelors: Masculinity, Girlhood, and Vision in the Art of Joseph Cornell and Henry Darger," PhD diss., University of California, Irvine, 2010 and "Many Stirring Scenes: Henry Darger's Reworking of American Visual Culture," *American Art* 26:1 (2012): 75–101.

55 My definition is drawn from "What Is the Definition of Intersex?" InterACT: Advocates for Intersex Youth, Sudbury, MA, Accessed June 18, 2020, www.interactadvocates.org/faq/#definition.

1 Littleness[1]

Little girls perform the personas of enslaved victim, warrior, heroine, and redeemer in *In the Realms of the Unreal*. Several volumes into his story, Henry Darger explains his preference for heroines:

> Although, dear readers, in this big story, boys and men play usual and principal parts in the dreadful battles, and during the great war encounter many terrible adventures, by land, sea, fire, water, and so forth, the reason the story runs so much with little girls as the actual heroes in this warfare is because, under most circumstances, women are braver than men. I go to show that by putting little girls in this story as the real heroines, that little girls do and are brave enough, for a fact, to be able to play and show any amount of nerve and courage, full equal or moreso (sic) than boys or men or women who may take part in active warfare.
>
> Of course, little girls and women have been seen to be a little nervous about small matters, like being frightened at a mouse or a spider, but not in all cases. I have known women who would, even bare-handed, catch a mouse. Also in the presence of real danger, when shells are bursting in the battlefield and shell fragments flying thickly, they have been known to be standing in the open field, looking for wounded to be brought in. What historian has not written in good and lengthy details of the heroism of the Red Cross Nurses and Sisters and other brave women? How about the play known as "The Little Rebel?" Was not she braver than the soldiers in that play?[2]

Moving from "small matters" of mice and spiders to "real dangers" of the battlefield, Darger expounds on the bravery of the female sex. Curiously, in this explanation he includes women, whom he largely omits from the rest of his story and imagery. Few adult women or mothers populate his tale, although, they exemplify superior constitutions over those of men. Darger's own mother died shortly after giving birth to his sister, who in turn, was given up by his father for adoption. The orphan child and themes of mother-less or broken families run throughout Darger's collection of children's lit-erature, in his stories, and in his personal history. Here, in this introductory passage, Darger specifically draws upon a surrogate maternal figure, the Red Cross Nurse and humanitarian icon of World War I. Strikingly monu-mental in propaganda posters and labeled "the greatest mother in the world," the nurse's visage evokes a secular Madonna in heavy drapery, enveloping a wounded, meek, and dispossessed soldier.[3] The mixture of altruism and Christian love exuding from this wartime icon aligns with the pious "Little Rebel"—Darger's other exemplar figure. This heroine of Edward Peple's 1911 play achieved widespread popularity through Shirley Temple's por-trayal in the major Hollywood production, "The Littlest Rebel" (1935). Negotiating the trials of the Civil War, this spunky Confederate belle epito-mizes fortitude and wholesomeness. Forced into a position of autonomy, motherless, and temporarily orphaned by the imprisonment of her father, the "Littlest Rebel" takes matters into her own hands. In the movie's climax, she appeals to Abraham Lincoln for the release of her father. The 6-year-old Miss Virgie, as pure as the white dresses she dons, orchestrates a heal-ing communion for all; the narrative closes as Yankees, Confederates, and slaves gather around the child in an embodiment of Christian forgiveness.

Darger's heroic example of "The Little Rebel" reflects an emerging pattern of self-sacrificing types that inform his re-conception of girlhood. Virginal and virtuous in thought, word, and deed, these girls suffer peril-ous journeys full of multiple trials, tragedies, and deaths testing their moral resolve. His fascination with this theme of child redeemers and martyrs appears throughout his literary and visual source material and becomes increasingly magnified in his artistic creations. Through such girl types, Darger constructs *littleness* (a blend of romantic Victorian childhood, girl saints, and floral Marian tropes) from such popular figures as the "Little Rebel," "Little Eva," and "The Little Flower of Christ." His admiration for, and creation of, little girl characters becomes the foundation of a develop-ing personal iconography in which he makes and re-makes his superlative child, the Vivian Girl.

Vivian

Although singular, Darger's "Vivian" favors the plural, possessing an amal-gam of secular looks and a polymorphous spirit that fuses with Catholic beliefs and practices. An early collage, one of Darger's first attempts to visually conjure the Vivians, offers insight into the development of his own heroic girls with eight appropriated, hand-colored reproductions (Figure 1.1).[4] According to Darger's story, seven sisters comprise the Vivian girls: Violet Mary Vivian, age 9½; Joice, age 10; Jennie, age 10; Evangeline (sometimes spelled as Angeline), age 9; Daisy, age 7; Hettie, age 8; and Catherine, age 7.[5] In this collage, the reproductions feature either commercial advertisements of dolls or portraits and genre scenes from eighteenth- and nineteenth-century fine art and popular culture sources, the most recognizable and outwardly pious being the supplicant boy, *The Infant Samuel Praying* (c. 1776) by Sir Joshua Reynolds. Popular imagery of girls by early twentieth-century illustrator Arthur John Elsley is also identifiable.[6] Captions underneath the portraits illuminate each girl's character and deeds. This composite of imagery and dramatic storytelling fashions an abbreviated saintly *vita* for each girl. For example, under Catherine Vivian (top left), the caption reads:

> Catherine Vivian was reported killed several times, but she was not. Yet some time during the early part of the Glandeco-Abbieannian War, her reported death was much disputed and found to be untrue as some else person was killed instead. Some at first said Abbieannians shot her to death by mistake, but in reality Glandelinians often tried to do it, but did not succeed. She is still very much *alive* (my emphasis).[7]

From this early work several governing leitmotifs and ambiguities surface, which continue throughout Darger's representation of the Vivians: their close proximity to death, their innocent nature, their ambiguous gender, and their iconic status. First, death, a sacrificial death that confirms

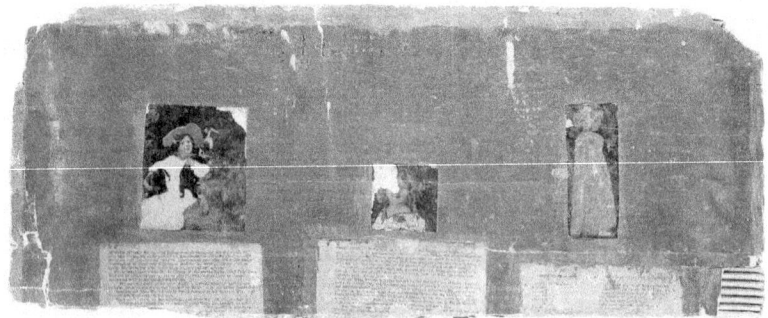

Figure 1.1 Henry Darger (1892–1973) © ARS, NY. Catherine Vivian, Violet Vivian, Joice Vivian, 1930–1972. Collage, watercolor, and type on paper 34.5 × 84.5 cm

life, lies not in Darger's narrative, but, prior to his tale, in the selection of the name "Vivian." The etymology of "Vivian" stems from the prefix *vivi-*, meaning "to enliven or animate." Figuratively suggestive of Darger's overall project—forcing what the artist calls as the "indescribable" into description—the girls come to life, become vivid, perceptible or real. Their passionate virtue and piety *vivifies* others, especially those fighting against evil. A deeper significance for "Vivian" lies in its Latin derivation, *vivam*, literally "I shall live,"[8] evoking an inextinguishable vitality that characterizes the Vivian Girls' demeanor and instinctual knack for survival. *Vivam* resembles a cry of resistance. Moreover, *vivam* resounds with a message of Christian resurrection and redemption embodied by the Vivian Girls in Darger's story.

Similarly, a Vivian trajectory of vitality, endurance, and dispossession echoes with a redundant declaration of persistent life within the name of Vivia Perpetua, the Catholic patron saint of mothers.[9] Martyred by Romans in 203 CE, St. Perpetua left behind an infant and a self-documented Passion detailing, not only her torments but also her visions. Venerated for her desire to suffer for the love of Christ, St. Perpetua holds the distinction of being one of seven women in the Eucharist prayer of Mass. She possesses another, more peculiar acclaim, as one of a few female saints performing a transcendence of her sex. Before the night of her martyrdom, Perpetua dreamt that she wrestled with an Egyptian and physically transforms. Her journal reads, "Then came out an Egyptian against me, of vicious appearance, together with his seconds, to fight me . . . my clothes were stripped off, and suddenly I was a man."[10] Darger's Vivians, likewise, sprout male genitalia during vulnerable and dramatic situations. As I argue in a following chapter, this is perhaps, more than a coincidence as their Vivian name and Vivia bodies radiate similar redemptive forces in saintly proportions and blur conventional gender boundaries throughout the *In the Realms of the Unreal*'s narrative. Their mysterious, queer ambiguity—betwixt and between that of a girl and boy—continually reinforces through a web of enchanting and subversive signifiers involving Vivian construction, meaning, and reception.

Indeterminate gender equally evolves from Darger's initial selection of fine art portraits in this early untitled collage representing the Vivians. Reynolds' *The Infant Samuel Praying (Samuel)* reflects its designated male gender in title; however, the image retains a gendered ambiguity and elevated countenance characteristic of what Anne Higonnet calls the "romantic child."[11] Sensuously portrayed with rosy cheeks, dimpled hands, wide eyes, and flowing hair, Samuel exudes angelic innocence and embodies an ideological Victorian construct of the "child." Formulated in the eighteenth-century writings of Jean-Jacques Rousseau and William Wordsworth, this developing concept of childhood valorized child innocence and celebrated the wisdom of self-directed natural growth and play. Circumventing sexuality and social inequality, the "child" represented a lost state separate from adulthood, a state that the child could restore in the hearts of adults.[12] According to Higonnet, "an older concept of a child born in Original sin, correctible through rigid discipline, hard work, and corporal punishment, gave way to a concept of the child born innocent of adult faults, social evils and sexuality."[13]

In the context of Darger's collage, *Samuel*'s indeterminate gender sets the stage for later iterations of Vivian girls. His shoulder length hair and white gown replicates with some variation on the other "girls." *Samuel*'s soulful expression and gentle manner reiterates looks and deportments of the other children. Little boy or little girl does not matter in this Vivian collage, as long as these portraits sustain the codes of innocence and sentiment that flavor Victorian childhood. Darger treats their images accordingly, like small treasures within a keepsake box; he isolates and savors them, one by one, in little cut-out rectangles. Like *Samuel* in his old-fashioned gown from centuries past, the collage's aging patina magically preserves a distant childhood, far removed from Darger's present.

One senses within this Vivian collage, replete with culturally coded innocence, the flow of nostalgic reverie unencumbered by the adult world. This flow ends abruptly when the visual collides with the adulterated violence of written text heralding the Vivians' war storm tales. Within this series of short paragraphs, Darger simultaneously transgresses and heightens the collage's significance as an artifact of holy childhood. Bourgeois, clean, and quiet appearances clash with captions of deadly exploits and engagements with blood-thirsty Glandelinians. The grim descriptions, even though incredulous, underscore a need to protect childhood and an elegiac tone inherent within individual pictures and the display as a whole. His fictional Vivian *vitas* function as small holy card icons, providing solitary figures and descriptive lives resembling the passion and resolution of saints. Instead of defining attributes, Darger equips his Vivians with powerful codes of feminine virtue: meekness, vulnerability, self-abnegation, and virginity.

According to scholar John M. MacGregor, this collage resided on Darger's "mimic altar" a sacred shrine through which Darger petitioned for the return of a misplaced newspaper photograph.[14] This image of 5-year-old Elsie Paroubek—abducted and murdered in Chicago—became a flashpoint of contention between the artist and his Catholic beliefs.[15] Darger's anxiety over this dead child also manifests in his art; Paroubek haunts his story as its first martyr, reappearing numerous times as a fleeting and beautiful apparition.[16] Unable to find the clipping, Darger repeatedly prayed for its return through divine intercession, but, without results:

> Storming heaven for the petition . . . [e]recting mimic altar to pray before, in order to obtain petition. . . . Sacrifices will be made for the granting of the petition. Making the mimic chapel neat and clean, no matter how much work. Buying materials of all sorts for shrine.[17]

Recording his frustrations within his journal, Darger indicates that he held high expectations for the intercessory powers of his homemade girl-icons, even though, suggesting their ersatz status as part of a "mimic" altar. At times frustrated with God for ignoring his requests, Darger admits to wanting to throw items at his icons.[18] The Vivian images on his mimic altar received similar treatment. After several months of petitioning for the lost photograph without results, he writes, "On August 1912 . . . Great loss in child pictures . . . altar thrown down."[19] These child pictures attest to Darger's inclusion of children's images in his practices of iconic veneration—aesthetic contemplation and petitioning, meticulous display and maintenance, and, even, occasions for violence and iconoclasm.[20]

The Vivian collage's thematic interplay of death and martyrdom, indeterminate gender, innocent virtue, and iconicity point toward a significant means of communication with divinity through the power of little girl imagery. Expropriating the "romantic child" from a popular culture context, Darger maps this child over analogous figures—fictitious warrior maidens—evocative of young women in Catholic hagiography. This mapping allows these two cultures to seamlessly correspond and coexist. Intricately weaving the secular and the sacred, text and image, and depiction and belief, Darger magically imbues these portraits with life; he vivifies them. *Still very much alive*, they hold meaning and a powerful presence.

The Little Flower

St. Thérèse of Lisieux (1873–1897), the self-proclaimed "The Little Flower of Christ," is widely known by Catholics. Canonized in 1925 while Darger wrote and illustrated *In the Realms of the Unreal*, this French "girl" saint was adored due to her girlish innocence and humble inspirations (coined the *little way* and published in 1925 as part of an autobiography). St. Thérèse rose to sainthood through a life of self-abnegation, virgin virtue, devotion to Christ, and visionary episodes. The writings of the Little Flower, in comparison to Darger's descriptions of the Vivians, read with a similar, highly sentimental, sticky sweet rhetoric (including an overuse of the adjective "little"), a moralizing tone modeled in female virtue, and an adolescent passion for Christ.[21] Thérèse's autobiography, *Histoire d'une Ame* (*Story of a Soul*, published in 1898, translated into twenty languages by 1925) chronicles her life and letters. As a postulant, she took the name "Thérèse of the Child Jesus and of the Holy Face." Later, she added the self-effacing title, "The Little Flower of Christ." St. Thérèse's call to figuratively stay unassuming and humble like little children, resonates throughout her writings as metaphors for loving Jesus and embracing martyrdom:

> Jesus has not said to us: "I am the flower of the gardens, the cultivated rose," but He tells us: "I am the flower of the fields and the Lily of the valleys." Jesus deigned to teach me this mystery. He set before me the book of nature, I understood how all the flowers He has created are beautiful, how the splendor of the rose and the whiteness of the Lily do not take away the perfume of the *little violet* or the delightful simplicity of the *daisy*. I understood that if all flowers wanted to be roses, nature would lose her springtime beauty, and the fields would no longer be decked out with the little wild flowers.
>
> And so it is in the world of souls, Jesus' garden, He willed to create great souls comparable to Lilies and roses, but He has created smaller ones and these must be content to be *daisies or violets* destined to give joy to God's glances when He looks down at his feet. Perfection consists in doing His will, in being what He wills us to be.[22] (italicized emphasis mine)

St. Thérèse's floral metaphors urge one to remain *little* or *childlike* in order to please Christ and retain immunity from adult corruptive forces. Dying in a convent at the young age of 22, her short and holy life represents what she espoused—an eternal spirit of girlhood describing dogmatic concepts in simple, childish terms of sunshine, blooming flowers, and smiling Madonnas. Theologians, however, argue that St. Thérèse's writings should not be dismissed as "Peter Pantheism," or a refusal to grow up.[23] Instead, her concepts express a practical dogma of re-creation and dependence upon God, the Father (often called "Papa" by St. Thérèse). This "divine adoption" commences at Baptism and continues forever, reinforced through the Sacraments. Remaining humble and childlike enables one to open his/her heart "to the transfiguring action of the Holy Spirit."[24] The *little way* confirms Christ's message in Matthew 18:3–4: "Verily I say unto you, Except ye be converted, and become as little children, ye shall not enter into the kingdom of heaven. Whosoever therefore shall humble himself as this little child, the same is greatest in the kingdom of heaven."[25]

Darger's awareness of the Little Flower is evident in his retention of two newsletters from the Society of the Little Flower, one published in 1932 and the other in 1959, a holy card of the saint, and two re-purposed letters from Catholic charities devoted to her.[26] More importantly, he demonstrates an understanding of the Little Flower's message and exemplar role by including St. Thérèse's image in *After the Battle of Drowsabella/ After Mr. Wirther Run/At Angeline Agatha* (Figure 1.2). In this work, he re-interprets her holy card as a large hanging painting. The card exhibits attributes of St. Thérèse: nun habit, a bouquet of roses held around a crucifix, and the presence of the Christ child. Thérèse's ample, doe-like eyes

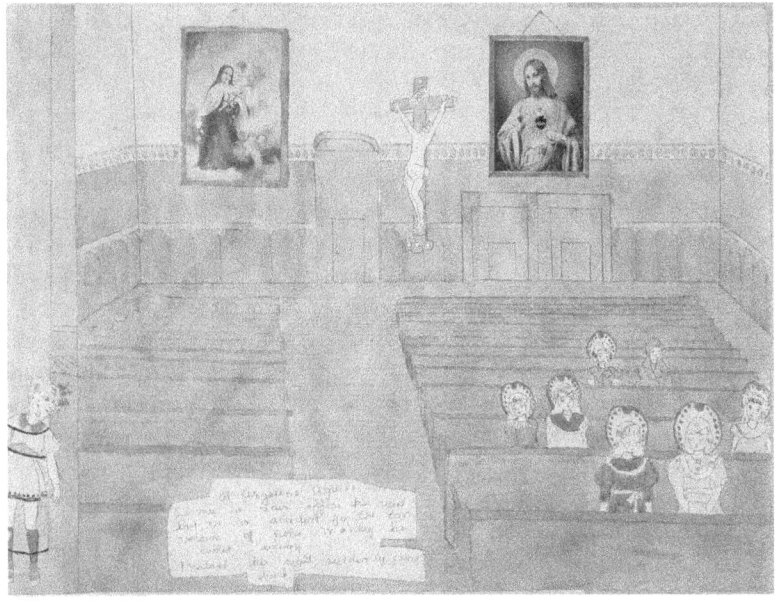

Figure 1.2 Henry Darger (1892–1973) © ARS, NY. After the Battle of Drowsabella/ After Mr. Wirther Run/At Angeline Agatha (recto); 39. At Jennie/ Richee./From the low stretch/of land from green hill/to left of this picture/they swim the ten mile/stretch of water to the land/seen to the left of/picture 38 where arrow/points (verso), n.d. Watercolor, gouache, black transfer carbon, graphite, and collage of cut-and-pasted printed elements, with pen and black ink (recto and verso), on three sheets of cream wove paper, pieced at left and right edges, with attached inscriptions 481 × 1,781 mm. Gift of Nathan Lerner, 1980.102

gaze upon a floating Christ-child apparition who, in turn, reciprocates her attention. Seraphim, too, watch this encounter magnifying the loving, child-like exchange between the Little Flower and her Christ.

Thérèse's image frames the upper left corner of Darger's composition, fortifying a *little way* subtext with its companion piece—a holy card of Christ. Reading clearly as a conventional "heart of Jesus" motif, Christ opens his tunic to reveal a flaming and thorn-bound heart radiating light. Signifying passion and sacrifice, this glowing emblem serves as a promi-nent, Catholic iconographic element in both Jesus and Mary imagery. In *After the Battle of Drowsabella/After Mr. Wirther Run/At Angeline Agatha*, the holy cards of Christ and St. Thérèse flank the artist's hand-drawn rendi-tion of a large crucifix; together this trio illustrates Christian self-sacrifice and passion through exemplars of male and female redemptive figures. Situated above the Vivian story unfolding before and beneath them, this powerful backdrop underscores the message of *little girl* virtue within the composition's full caption: *At Angelina Agatha. Jennie in vain offers her sight lost in an accident for the conversion of John Manley her worst enemy. Instead her sight suddenly came back.*

Offering up her ability to see for the good of the Christian cause, Jen-nie Vivian performs an act in accordance with those of confessor saints like St. Thérèse, desiring to give of herself in order to cleanse the sins of others. Sitting in church pews, the Vivians pray. With tear-stained cheeks and closed eyes, their faces reflect either calm acceptance or a slight frowning distress. Most wear wide-brim, yellow hats with red trim and red dots accents. Each brim encircles their heads reminiscent of adorn-ing frames surrounding iconic imagery on Catholic devotional scapulars. Only the open eyes of St. Thérèse and Christ engage those of the viewer, reinforcing their protective watch over the Vivians (and perhaps, over the viewer).

The Little Flower's inclusion in this work lends for erudite followers of Catholic faith a support structure of Christian virtue, self-sacrifice, and hope. St. Thérèse's presence contextualizes the Vivians within the *little way* of girl sainthood and popular philosophical belief exalting childhood as a redemptive force exemplified within the life of Christ. In this context, Darger's art responds, in part, to the tenor of the times, perhaps even to Pope Pius X declaration that "There will be saints among children!"[27]

Daisies and Violets

Two of the seven Vivian Girls have floral names: Violet Vivian and Daisy Vivian—the very humble flowers that St. Thèrése celebrates, those "des-tined to give joy to God's glances." During St. Thérèse's and Darger's lifetimes, violets and daisies held special significance in Victorian popular culture and in Catholic lore as emblems in "Mary Gardens." Whether secular or mystical, the symbolic content of gardens affirmed society's designation of gardens as feminine spaces and sites of domesticity. Accordingly, flowers provided abundant source material for expressing gender characteristics and qualities upheld in bourgeois culture, deifying motherly nurture and feminine virtues attributed to the Virgin Mary. Originating in Medieval tapestries and illuminated manuscripts, enclosed gardens, replete with fountains, flowers, and beasts, evolved as Marian iconography, expressing the life cycle of the Virgin or, specifically, serving as pictorial analogues to garden Annunciations. At times incorporating unicorns and phoenixes, these fantastic scenes served as poetic devices that mixed exotic metaphors and Biblical details into a compressed litany of praise. Interpretations of these images often cite the sensuous rhetoric of the Old Testament's Song of Solomon 4:12 celebrating pre-nuptial virginity and fidelity: "A garden enclosed is my sister, my spouse; a spring shut up, a fountain sealed."[28]

Violets and daisies frequent the enclosed garden motif, as well as Annunciation and Nativity scenes. Standing for faithfulness, humility, and chastity, violets appropriately capture Mary's humble acceptance of her role.[29] The daisy's sweet simplicity symbolizes the innocence of the Christ Child and, according to legend, its star-like shape graced the entrance to the manger pointing the wise men toward the Nativity.[30] Both daisies and violets sprout up beneath the feet of the Virgin within the enclosed garden. St. Thérèse's *little way,* extolling the value of these common flowers, presents a microcosm of Mary's Garden, a miniaturization of the enclosed space— even smaller and humbler in significance—and its metaphors of virginity and submission. As Thérèse capitalizes on these associations, Darger, likewise, draws from floral symbolism to underscore Violet Vivian's goodness as she explains her nickname Susan and real name, Violet:

> I so often go after the flowers called Black eye Susans they are so pretty on a Church Altar. I love all flowers but more so the beautiful Violets and Forget me nots. . . . I always had the joy of finding huge clusters of the fragrant sweet smelling violets hidden away under the hedges of a Country lane, and using them for to decorate my room or for the Altars which of course brought me to have the real name of Violet, for Violet is a meaning of humility.[31]

Guiding the Vivians through perilous situations and adventures, Violet Vivian embodies the Christian ideal of meek and humble leadership. Daisy Vivian, in comparison, abounds with energy, a "wildcat" who "wins renown by doing dangerous stunts, and giving tit for tat."[32] Her rambunctious nature tailors to Darger's favorite "Little Rebel." The association between Daisy and precocious, rebellious girls is, perhaps, not coincidental on Darger's part. Juliette Gordon Low (1860–1927) (affectionately known as "Daisy") achieved notoriety as founder of the Girl Scouts of America in 1912, the same year that Darger fabricated his "mimic altar." Biographers, noting that Daisy Low was the daughter of a Confederate officer, nickname her "The Little Rebel."[33] Self-reliant and resourceful, Low exemplified qualities she espoused to young girls eager for outdoor experiences and skills previously taught to young boys. In addition to gender-specific homemaking lessons, early Girl Scout manuals provided information on shooting guns, riding horses, and surviving in the wild.[34] With these associations in mind, Daisy and Violet, the courageous tomboy and the patient leader, respectively, define Vivian Girl temperaments and values. They adequately frame Darger's imaginary childhood as aesthetic ideals exhibiting a sacred virtue and subversive female independence.

One of Darger's numerous garden scenes, *Untitled* (Figure 1.3), conflates little bodies and floral symbolism with vigor, as if the artist engages his own visual vocabulary in dialogue with St. Thérèse's Marian tropes and ideology. Because of the prevalence of similar scenes in Darger's mature work (from 1944 on), this discussion treats them as a type or particular motif. Garden scenes share distinct characteristics: pastoral settings, frontal depiction of girls, attentive eye contact, exuberant decoration and patterning (flowers, polka dots, flocking birds), lack of movement, and no obvious visual narrative cues or captions. Messages of metaphoric blooming and innocence arise in these scenes with their clumping replication of girls, emphasis on facial visibility, and overabundance of flora.

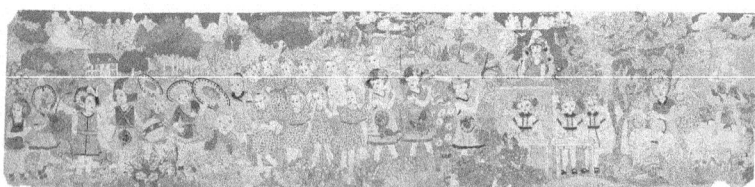

Figure 1.3 Henry Darger (1892–1973) © ARS, NY. Untitled (double-sided), mid-twentieth century. Watercolor, pencil, carbon tracing, and collage on pieced paper 24 × 106 ½". Museum purchase with funds generously provided by John and Margaret Robson © Kiyoko Lerner 2004.1.3B

In *Untitled*, flower after flower willingly open their petals, exposing dainty internal centers; they orient these multiple faces, like those of the girls, toward the foreground and the viewer's gaze. Their centers, small and round, echo the shape and scale of polka dots, assorted buttons, hat embellishments, and black hole eyes that punctuate girls' bodies. These elements merge into one densely packed, mesmerizing and reverberating pattern of girlish energy throughout the composition. This lush compaction exudes a collective effervescence, a fecund bliss, available, waiting, and attentive to the beholder.

A corresponding portraiture between bloom and little girl emerges with greater emphasis from the middle of this composition. Three repeating girls, each holding either a cowboy boot or rose, twist their bodies in an unnatural *contrapossto* allowing adequate display of both their faces and the rhythmic motif of pansy–passion flower-pansy on their skirts. Standing out as the only collaged elements among a mass of traced imagery, these pansy–passion flower motifs present a single bloom—some with the addition of a leaf or two, full and frontal.[35] The pansy, in particular, multiplies the significance of adorable faces (and faces for adoration) through association with the human face.[36] Girl faces and flower faces align at consistent heights like points along a rectangular schema directing one's gaze in a loop of upper body to lower body connect-the-dots. In composing this work, Darger wrought frenzied patterns of clustering, overlapping, and polka-dotting bodies; he slows the composition down within this segment, offering a contemplative space for formal and metaphoric comparison between flower and face.

The relevance of the pansy and passion flower duo figuratively expands in this seemingly disparate juxtaposition. Both flowers hold prominence in Catholic iconography regarding the life of Christ. Of the two, the passion flower retains more notoriety as symbolic of Christ's sacrifice while the pansy's inner trefoil patch of contrasting color evokes the Trinity.[37] Additionally, the placement of these flowers on the girls' skirts conveys, perhaps, more than just decorative fashion. Each noticeably covers the little girl's genital region and, thus, symbolically overlays the sacrificial martyrdom of Christ (passion flower) and the purity of the Immaculate Conception (pansy) on the virginal girl body. In this pulsing loop of face-bloom–sanctity–virginity, Darger declares and constructs a sacred maidenhead.

Floral tropes and religious overtones continually inscribe the Vivians' bodies with similar loops of face-bloom in related garden scenes. Pansies cover genital areas while clumping daisies, black-eyed Susans, lilies, and roses additionally wrap around the little girls' legs and torsos. Those flowers, appearing much larger than the girls, reinforce their diminutive littleness while providing an imaginative sense of childish scale. Likewise, in

Darger's text, flowers and Vivians intertwine. One passage, for instance, links them through olfactory exuberance. Transfiguring after surviving a mine explosion, the Vivians emit a scent akin to an unearthly perfume. Apparently, divinity smells like flowers. Darger writes:

> As he (Jack Evans) proceeded on, he saw sitting on the porch four fair little girls, really ten times more beautiful than the Vivian girls could ever have been. . . . Then he paused in overpowering emotion and awe, for from these pretty children a strange fragrance as of the most sweetest flowers, a strange odor that was completely divine, that filled the air. . . . Oh, Evans dear, you have come back! . . . We are your beautiful friends called the 'Vivian Girls,' and we have recovered from the mine explosion, and are not disfigured, blind, or crippled.[38]

Within this language of flowers, in particular when speaking of blooms, one also whispers inevitable "death." Transient beauty and fragility underscore the flower's precious appeal, making the flower ever so sweet and wistful. An adept metaphor for "the child" or St. Thèrése's spiritual littleness, the flower emits a simultaneous beauty and vulnerability, which, although *lowly and insignificant*, conjures desire and eroticizes speech in potent ways. Even St. Thérèse's rhetoric cannot escape this duality:

> Jesus and the angels who, like the vigilant bees, know how to gather the honey contained within the mysterious and multiple calyxes that represent souls or rather the children of the virginal little flower . . . when a flower has blossomed, we have only to pluck it, but when and how will Jesus pluck His little flower? . . . Perhaps the pink color of its corolla indicates that this will be by means of martyrdom! . . . Yes, I feel my desires are reborn. Perhaps after having asked us love for love, so to speak, Jesus will want to ask us blood for blood, life for life. . .[39]

"Plucking" the flower-virgins and gathering honey from "mysterious calyxes" reads precariously like euphemisms for sexual intercourse. Cultural historian Marina Warner eloquently relays these fluid correspondences between flowers, virginity, and martyrdom in her history of Joan of Arc.[40] She traces the specific name Joan adopted, "Jehanne la Pucelle," through its etymology of *pucelle*, meaning a particular shade of "virgin" ambiguously defined by both innocence and nubility, to the Middle Age's *despulceler*, "to deflower."[41] *Pucelle*, Warner argues, connotes a transitional state, ripe with promise and sexual becoming.[42] Like St. Joan, the Little Flower anticipates her martyrdom and subsequent metaphoric defloration or ascension as Christ's bride into heaven.[43] She humbly waits, signaling her receptivity by becoming pink for her divine Sun:

> [T]heir pink corollas are turned in the direction of the dawn, they are awaiting the rising of the sun; as soon as this radiant star has sent toward them its warm rays, the timid little flowers open up their calyxes,[44] and their dainty leaves form a sort of crown which, uncovering their little yellow hearts. . . . Throughout the whole day, the daisies do not cease gazing on the sun, and they turn like it until the evening . . . Jesus is the divine Sun, and the daisies are His spouses, the virgins[45]
>
> Perhaps, in the evening of its life, the daisy will offer the divine Spouse its corolla, become pink.[46]

The Little Flower's floral metaphors and desires ring familiar with narratives of similar pious virgins in Catholic lore, pining for Christ and their heavenly nuptial chambers.[47] Imagining herself as a crown daisy, like the many beneath the Virgin's feet in Mary Garden imagery, this little flower awaits her spiritual bridegroom. Her chaste body exists in a state of expectancy; a matrix of desires and denials mapping across her allegorical form. In her childish little way, the color pink—the baby of red—replaces the sanguinary symbolism of martyr's blood and, instead, inadvertently references a coquettish, warm blush on the flower-virgin face. Given their virtuous demeanor and narrative role as martyrs (either slaves or participants in the slave rebellion), the girls in Darger's garden imagery play into Catholic conventions of virgin martyrs as they wait for martyrdom, turning their faces in accordance with other "little flowers" in Jesus' wake.[48]

The inherent innocence and virtue of a child's perspective coupled with religious overtones displaces eroticism in the writings of the Little Flower. Darger shares a similar talent for description that teasingly evades, yet, also invites sexuality. Perhaps because his words, like his images, construct a protective coating of *littleness* correlating with authoritative secular and religious models, he seems unaware of its sensual power. Or, on the other hand, he revels within its sensual power for *littleness* offers a safe space capable of regulating his fantasies. Nonetheless, his words insist that the Vivians remain unquestionably pure, as if their excessive girlishness defies all corruption and corrosion. He describes them in glowing terms:

> Every one of the Vivian Girls has so sweet a temper, and ways more charming than their beauty, that they were the greatest pleasure to all the nation. . . . No artist could paint them correctly. They had soft fine golden hair which could curl up beautifully, or which they could wear in any fashion they chose; they had big blue eyes and long eyelashes,

and the most darling little faces. They were strong and sturdy for their ages, and were such expert horseback riders that they could do all the stunts observed at a circus on horseback. Their manners were so good that it was like a heavenly delight to make their acquaintance. They felt that everyone was their friend, and when anyone spoke to them, they would give the stranger one serious sweet look with their blue eyes, and then follow it with a lovely and most friendly kind of smile. . . . when dressed as boys, yet still retaining their golden curls, they looked like seven beautiful Little Lord Fauntleroys, with a wealth of naturally curly hair of eighteen-carat-gold shade.

Yet, despite all their beauty and equal goodness, they had often proved to the persecuting Glandelinians that they were more than a match for them.[49]

Elsewhere, the Vivians receive similar praise by Jack Evans, a Christian soldier and chaperone of the girls:

Indeed for my part, human language is utterly inadequate to express the beauty of the Vivian Girls. The supreme loveliness of the celestial spirits, as it seems to me, is nothing compared with the Vivian Girls, who far surpass everything that is pleasing to our mortal eyes. How exquisitely beautiful are the blue vaulted heavens, when it is studded with so many stars like so many sparkling gems. All natural beauty and grandeur grows dim when compared to the charm and magnificence of the starry heavens on a tranquil summer night. Beautiful is the sun, which because of its wonderful splendor and radiance, was adored as a divine being by so many pagan nations. But more beautiful is the form of the Vivian Girls. When I accompanied them through the streets of the Abbieannian towns, the little girls were so attractive that people flocked around to gaze at their lovely features, and the mere sight of them turned mere sadness into joy and love.[50]

In both of these descriptions, the Vivians exceed even the beauty of the heavens yet, exhibit conventional markers of Victorian bourgeois child prettiness—curly blonde hair and blue eyes. Caught in a slippage between flirtatious, innocent types (Shirley Temple) and celestial creatures (angels and cherubs), the Vivian descriptions tease with claims of an inadequacy to capture their visage while expounding with sensuous elaborations on hair and features that beg the reader to imagine their mesmerizing beauty in familiar terms. All the while, these exaltations of physical enchantment intermix with a tomboyishness underscoring the Vivians' toughness, strength, and sweet temper.

For Darger, these Vivian attributes transfer effortlessly through visual culture. His little girls originate in eighteenth-century child portraits and reconfigure in imagery he culls from modern-day comic strips, fashion illustration, and coloring books (c. 1915–1970). These plucky, girl types replace the "romantic child" of early collages taking on a revisionist modern girlhood—boisterous, parentless, physical and adventuresome. Still blonde-haired, blue-eyed and prepubescent, these new Vivians animate their name through bodily language and actions; they run, ride horses, and shoot guns. Very little differentiation exists in their appearances, and for that matter, between them and the other girls populating *In the Realms of the Unreal*, some wear pigtails; others sport pageboy haircuts or shoulder length bobs. Sometimes two or three Vivians look younger—plumper and shorter—than the group. Visually they mimic each other, just as their girl counterparts appear to replicate in Darger's art. Only the Vivians' cohesive uniforms, blonde hair, tendency to grouping, and number (totaling seven) distinguish them from girl slaves.[51] Repetitions of exact or similar looking girls (Caucasian, blonde-haired, and blue-eyed) swell throughout Darger's images and text like incantations. Belaboring their attributes of conventional beauty, he attempts to enchant the reader/viewer with reiteration and reinforcement of an ideal, white middle class appearance. Divinity and pop culture weave together inextricably in Darger's conception of heroic girlhood—well-dressed, self-motivated, devout, pure—maidens plucked for service, destined to transfigure into martyrs and transcend into spiritual victory.

Dying *Little*, Returning Home

> Whoever is a LITTLE ONE, let him come to me
>
> —Proverbs 9:4[52]

Darger's devotion to *littleness* expands beyond the *Little Way*'s many virtues and metaphors that St. Thérèse extols. Little characters proliferate his collection of children's literature and exemplify his standard for heroines. "The Little Rebel" type, for example, follows in the footsteps of a burgeoning genre of juvenile war literature during and following the American Civil War. These adventure war novels invited children to imagine themselves within the ranks of spies, scouts, and drum corps. Child protagonists stepped outside of their normative roles due to disruptions in their family structure and home life. As the war placed more demands upon the home front, these stories allowed children to vicariously become involved, connecting the notions of broken family with broken nation. In many tales, the child served to bridge political and racial gaps, bringing together adults separated by conflict. Girls were not exempt from these patriotic and outwardly Christian texts that promoted individual virtue and character.[53] Often portrayed as orphans, thus, justifying their decision to leave home, girls and young women, like the protagonist of the "Little Rebel," exhibit a potentially subversive persona—a powerful female child/youth outside the family structure, a tomboyish adventurer rebelling against social and gendered norms. These children's adventure stories of the early to mid-1860s preceded a wave of turn-of-the-century novels involving child protagonists. Darger's collection of literature included many famous examples of child adventurers from mid-nineteenth century to the early twentieth, including: L. Frank Baum's *Wizard of Oz* series, Johanna Spyri's *Heidi*, Robert Louis Stevenson's *Kidnapped*, J.M. Barrie's *Peter Pan*, Charles Dicken's *The Old Curiosity Shop* and *Oliver Twist*, and Mark Twain's *The Adventures of Huckleberry Finn*.

Diminutive ones held special, even venerated status in most of these mid and turn-of-the-century novels. Perhaps too pure for earthly existence, many little characters died tragically, their highly sentimental deathbed scenes connecting with readers through shared emotions of suffering and loss. Death selfishly clings to this cult of littleness, yet, holds only a temporary power akin to suspended animation, as with Dickens' Little Nell, who on her passing "seemed a creature fresh from the hand of God, and waiting for the breath of life."[54] The Vivian, conceptualized by Darger within a visual culture celebrating and longing for children, declares "I shall live," as a form of resistance, a powerful figure that both follows and transgresses norms, and, at times, transcends them.

Perhaps no other little girl's figure of nineteenth-century culture dies so well and with such saintly aplomb as Little Eva (Evangeline St. Clare) of Harriet Beecher Stowe's *Uncle Tom's Cabin, or, Life Among the Lowly* (1852). The importance of this abolitionist novel and Stowe's girl protagonist permeates Darger's narrative and construction of the Vivians. Darger openly appropriates the novel's religious rhetoric, attitudes toward slavery, and character typology. He greatly favors Little Eva, who he uses as a measuring stick for Christian love and morality in descriptions of his own Vivians. He writes:

> Of Violet, Joice, Jennie and Evangeline, their beauty could never be described, but their nature and ways of goodness and soul was still more pretty and spotless. And no Evangeline St. Clare could beat them in their kind loving ways, and their love for God. They were always willing to do as they were told, keeping away from bad company and going to Mass and Holy Communion every day, and living the lives of little saints.[55]

Little Eva performs as Stowe's Christ-like girl-child, a blonde-headed, blue-eyed innocent, famous for comforting her slave, Uncle Tom, with flower necklaces, tender caresses, and readings from the New Testament. Her steadfast Christian faith and charity moves her father to confront his own apathetic racism and heals the damaged soul of the incorrigible slave girl, Topsy. Darger's high esteem for the moral character of Little Eva, and for the religious appeal of Stowe's novel is apparent throughout the *In the Realms of the Unreal*.[56] Revised appropriations of whole paragraphs[57] and significant phrases from *Uncle Tom's Cabin* disseminate Darger's text, one of the more compelling examples being Simon Legree's retort to Uncle Tom, "An't yer mine, now, body and soul?" revisited by Darger as Jack Evans' question "Ain't those little girls mine to protect, body and soul?"[58] Both questions suggest possession and power, although Darger's revision inverts the entitlement of slave ownership Stowe's evil protagonist expresses turning Darger's retort into a statement of protection by abolitionist and Christian soldier, Jack Evans.

Little Eva's death and her life, as well as her beauty symbolize spiritual perfection. Stowe illuminates Little Eva as an object of veneration, describing her as "Always dressed in white, she seemed to move like a shadow through all sorts of places, without contracting spot or stain."[59] This euphemism of cleanliness pertains to Eva's moral purity. She is without sin. Although a Calvinist, Stowe aligns Little Eva's early death within that of Catholic girl saints, symbolically acting out a particular martyrdom of maidens—the preservation of her virginity. Dying in a prepubescent state, Little Eva retains an extreme purity untouched by sexuality and the suffering of menstruation.[60] Her body models the look and spirit of the Vivians—white, blonde, blue-eyed (sometimes wide eyed and pupils dilated)—signifying affluence and a prelapsarian state of grace.

Little Eva, in fact, serves as such a strong analogue for the Vivians that Darger actually resurrects her character. He writes in Volume I:

'Who are you little girl?' asked general Roswell Buster Johnston. 'What do you want in our lines?' The child looked reproachfully at the generals, and said, 'My name is Evangeline St. Clare, I have just escaped from the Glandelinians. . . . Sure you must have come from heaven.' Said general Hanson. 'Did you not die from consumption?' 'I nearly did, though the story about me says I did. I did not die, but fainted when the sickness got at its worse.' (BEG PARDON TO THE WRITER OF UNCLE TOM'S CABIN).[61]

In a sense, Darger *vivifies* Little Eva. Eva shall live. Regardless of his revision and apology to Stowe, Eva's death still lingers in *In the Realms of the*

Unreal. Her death surfaces as a paradigm for child death, suggesting the fading child's potential as a liminal space through which the reader vicariously experiences and visualizes heaven. The deathbed scene of Little Eva marks this Christian apex in Stowe's novel:

> On the face of the child, however, there was no ghastly imprint, only a high and almost sublime expression, the overshadowing presence of spiritual natures, the dawning of immortal life in that childish soul. . . . A bright, a glorious smile passed over her face, and she said, brokenly, 'O! love,—joy,—peace!' gave one sigh and passed from death unto life! Farewell, beloved child! the bright eternal doors have closed after thee.[62]

In their final moments, Darger's little girls also forgo their earthly bodies and gaze upon heaven. Severely mangled by storm wreckage, little Jennie Turmer tells the Vivians, "I'm going to Jesus, and mama in heaven now, and I hope you my dear friends to stay good so that we will see each other again in heaven." Jennie, after embracing them all, emits a cry of "heavenly joy, long to be remembered, 'OH, I SEE GOD.'"[63] And, a few pages later in the same volume, Darger recounts a gruesome martyrdom of an anonymous girl slave:

> A little girl was first brought out of the line of children, and was cruelly cut by awful knives. Her life blood trickled gently but in streams, from her sliced body, and then she bowed her head, and her pretty curls fell forward. Then the murderers ripped her body open, and she threw up her bloody arms and with a cry of, "I SEE GOD," fell limply backward dead but an unearthly happiness overspread her face and she seemed transfigured.[64]

Both passages exploit the symbolic power of *littleness*, using this privileged physical state, always already pure and destined for heaven, to compound martyred suffering. Darger's production of *littleness* operates in a similar manner to theorist Susan Stewart's notion of the miniature—a metaphoric embodiment of a world,

> not necessarily known through the senses, or lived experience. The child continually enters here as a metaphor, perhaps not simple because the child is in some physical sense a miniature of the adult, but also because the world of childhood, limited in physical scope yet fantastic in its content, presents in some way a miniature and fictive chapter in each life history. . . . We imagine childhood as if it were at the other end of a tunnel—distanced, diminutive, and clearly framed.[65]

Darger's girls, especially the Vivians, radiate with a similar kind of trans-cendent, implausible capacity. More than merely nostalgic notions, girls become warriors within his fictional tableau. Through the diminutive, effu-sively theatrical little girl body, Darger claims accessibility to mystic, secret realms. The horror of severing the mother–child bond, a driving abolitionist message and empathy-producing device in *Uncle Tom's Cabin*, comes forth with graphic intensity as bodily trauma and dismemberment to girl slaves in Darger's spectacles of martyrdom. Wounds spill forth messages of mother–child rupture and irrevocable familial damage while simultaneously evoking the ecstatic penetrations of visionary experiences and forthcoming healing. "Going to Jesus and Mama" the orphan-child Jennie returns "home," mak-ing her divine adoption complete. She, like the Little Flower, finds her fam-ily within her religious piety, and, accordingly, reassurance that they all will become one, again.[66] Dismembered bodies (families) transfigure whole. The brutally murdered child slave with streaming blood and fallen curls, like the Paschal Lamb, resigns herself to her sacrificial role. "Seeing God" she also returns to the fold.

To go home, one must follow the *little way* of saintly sacrifice. For Little Eva, her expression of saintliness manifests in confession—yearning to be like Christ:

> ... when I saw those poor creatures on the boat ... some had lost their mothers, and some their husbands, and some mothers cried for their lit-tle children. .... I've felt that I would be glad to die, if my dying could stop all this misery. I *would die* for them, Tom, if I could.[67]

Darger's girls, in extreme contrast, physically perform their imitation of Christ through the body, illuminating their physical suffering by mimick-ing his Passion compounding it with the Passions of every saint that has ever been eviscerated, bound, blinded, or scourged. Affirming the visual power of the broken body, these modern-looking girls slip into Medieval conventions of saintly acts. Darger's anachronistic method of depicting lit-tle girl sanctity heavily favors somatic evidence of suffering as a prelude to miracles or Resurrection. Wearing their *passio* and signs of sainthood on the body, his girls display the heinous acts and sins of others—*sacrifices that men would think of in horror*—taken to and beyond limits of hagiographic conventions, exceeding visual comfort levels and description.

Nowhere is this more apparent than in Darger's grotesque fantasies of martyrdom, where seeing the little girl body becomes even more crucial. Extreme crucifixions, disembowelments, and gore become necessary in his quest to articulate the intensity of spiritual release. In the center panel of a larger work, *At Norma Catherine via Jennie Richee, Vivian girls witness*

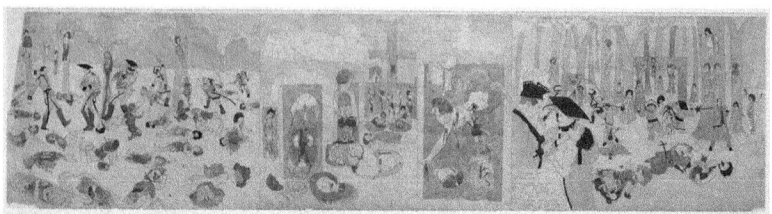

Figure 1.4 Henry Darger (1892–1973) © ARS, NY (a) Are almost murdered themselves though they fight for their lives typhoon saves them . . . b) Vivian girls said Glandelinian tent. (n.d.). Watercolor and pencil on paper
22 × 88" (55.9 × 223.5 cm). Gift of the artist's estate in honor of Klaus
Biesenbach. The Museum of Modern Art, New York, NY, U.S.A.

Source: Digital Image © The Museum of Modern Art/Licensed by SCALA/Art Resource, NY
© 2020 Kiyoko Lerner/Artists Rights Society (ARS), New York

children's (sic) bowels and other entrails torn out by infuriated Glandelin-
ians. The result after the massacre. Only a few of the murdered children
are shown here (Figure 1.4). Children essentially turn into specimens for
dissection. Several torn bodies hang from panels embedded in the ground.
Disembodied heads riddle the landscape along with crosses displaying crucified girls. Blood and gore are everywhere. Such gratuitous violence overwhelms any sense of meaning or spiritual elevation.

Numerous other martyrdom scenes, engrossing the viewer/reader in grand
scales of violence exponentially intensify this heavy, corporeal gaze. Most
scholars, unsurprisingly, find this repetition of horrific death unnerving.
Some even use it to suggest evidence of psychosis, claiming that Darger's
art springs "from the mind of a serial killer."[68] Sporadic additions of male
genitalia on living and martyred girls further complicate readings of such
scenes and additionally urge calls for psychoanalytic interpretations. Darger's art of excessive little girl bodies reconfigures martyrdom by fearlessly
transforming the little female body to combat socio-political constructs and
(over) exposing her flesh as raw, visceral sacrifice to the precarious extent
of becoming profane, meaningless carnage. Excessive bodily representation
slips along an axis of sacred and prurient possibilities.

Whether or not viewers consider Darger's child martyrdoms pointless,
obscene, or even pornographic, and whether or not their intensity holds an
erotic charge for the artist, these images, nevertheless, are relevant to the
manner in which he constructs holiness and wholeness. Little girls' bodies
display Christian sacrifice viscerally, inferring through their inherent purity
that they, like Christ, suffer the sins of others. Created concurrently with the

blooming garden works (c. 1944–1960s), these explicit martyrdom scenes convey similar messages with divergent visual means. One provides brutal evidence of violent suffering while the other allegorizes martyrdom through symbolic *little ways*—miniature Marian gardens full of expectant blooms and virginal sacrifice. Each plays off the other in an entangling map of Christian ideals: Marian conventions, *little* girl sainthood, and *imitatio Christi*.

Acknowledging this, one can begin to see the little girl as a powerful multivalent and formulaic abstraction blooming (literally) everywhere in Darger's art. Modeling his little heroines after a bevy of rebellious, orphaned girls and virtuous female martyrs, Darger understood girlhood in his story as a journey of suffering and self-abnegation. A living *vivam* image of redemption, she represents a sacred body and, as such, must show the marks of sacrifice in her broken and glorious flesh. Comic and coloring book quotations provide her form, while also reinforcing her humble status as an ordinary and banal child destined to do wondrous deeds. Simultaneously familiar and strange, her image constantly shifts, transfiguring the innocent and vulnerable Victorian-to-modern-child into a militarized, impassioned (little) Joan of Arc that Darger retrofits in polka dots and patent leather shoes. Her alluring body performs a circle of life to death to life, a heated existence teeming with vitality and innocence. Betwixt and between, her liminal, martyred, and indeterminate form animates Darger's heterodoxical vision driven by an ambivalent dialogue between the sacred and the profane. The *little* girl is Darger's pious vessel, a compressing narrative of womb and tomb, a flowing desire. She remains, still, *very much alive*.

Notes

1 Portions of this chapter were previously published in Leisa Rundquist, "Little Ways: Girlhood According to Henry Darger," *Southeastern College Art Conference Review* XV:4 (2009): 434–447. The current chapter contains modifications and updates.
2 Darger, *In the Realms of the Unreal*, 262–263.
3 This particular poster with the text, "The Greatest Mother in the World" was created by illustrator, A.E. Foringer in 1918.
4 The upper and lower registers of this collage are no longer together. The upper section is part of the Collection de l'art Brut in Lausanne, Switzerland. The author was unable to locate the lower portion of this collage at the time of publication. Full images of this collage can be found in MacGregor, *In the Realms of the Unreal*, 146 and the author's article: Rundquist, "Little Ways: Girlhood According to Henry Darger," 435.
5 Although there is no indication that Darger modeled his Violet from a known individual, Violet Mary Vivian, M.B.E. (1879–1962) was a contemporary to the artist. She was the daughter of Baron Crespigny Vivian, a British diplomat.
6 These include "Wake Up! It's Christmas!" (1909) and "Which May I Keep?" (1901). Both feature little girls around the same age as the Vivians. One

represents a bedroom scene where a girl is being woken up by a woman and dog. The other shows a girl in bonnet and flowing gown having a conversation with a St. Bernard about the puppies she holds.

7 Catherine Vivian caption from the upper portion of the Vivian collage. This particular paragraph ends with "She is also one of the pretty girl Vivian Girl Princesses as innocent as innocent can be, and as pure hearted, and as brave as a saint, and serves well in Abbieannia's Holy Cause." Henry Darger, *Catherine Vivian, Violet Vivian, Joice Vivian* (1930–1972) collage, watercolor, and type on paper 34.5 × 84.5 cm, photo: Claude Bornand, Collection de l'Art Brut, Lausanne no inv. cab-11555, © 2020 Kiyoko Lerner/Artists Rights Society (ARS), New York.

8 Marina Warner cites the English translation of *vivam* in *Fantastic Metamorphosis: Other Worlds: Ways of Telling the Self* (New York: Oxford University Press, 2002), 16. Latin translations of *vivus* and aforementioned derivatives also at Kevin Cawley, "Latin Dictionary and Grammar Aid," accessed January 10, 2014, http://catholic.archives.nd.edu/latgramm.htm.

9 "Vivia" also appears as "Vibia" in some hagiographies.

10 L. Stephanie Cobb, *Dying to Be Men: Gender and Language in Early Christian Martyr Texts* (New York: Columbia University Press, 2008), 105.

11 Anne Higonnet, *Pictures of Innocence: The History and Crisis of Ideal Childhood* (London: Thames and Hudson, 1988), 22.

12 Such romanticized notions still inform how we understand childhood today—pure, innocent, and separate from adulthood. For extended discussions on cultural constructions of childhood, see Philippe Ariès, *Centuries of Childhood: A Social History of Family Life*, trans. Robert Baldick (New York: Vintage Books, 1962); and Marilyn R. Brown, ed. *Picturing Children: Constructions of Childhood between Rousseau and Freud* (Burlington, VT: Ashgate Publishing, 2002).

13 Higonnet, *Pictures of Innocence*, 26.

14 MacGregor theorizes that this particular collage resided on Darger's mimic altar. He attributes it to Darger's early work due to the type of imagery, collaging methods, and aged appearance. MacGregor, *In the Realms of the Unreal*, 146–148.

15 Both Bonesteel and MacGregor interpret Darger's fixation on Elsie Paroubek's missing photograph as a psychotic break from reality. According to Bonesteel, Darger's incorporation of his search for this photograph as the "Aronburg Mystery" in *In the Realms of the Unreal* text marked the "first indication that Darger has stepped across the line between reality and fantasy." See Bonesteel, *Henry Darger*, 10–11 and MacGregor, *In the Realms of the Unreal*, 494–519.

16 According to MacGregor and Bonesteel, Elsie Paroubek materializes in Darger's story as Annie Aronburg, a child rebel leader assassinated by the Glandelinians. MacGregor, *In the Realms of the Unreal*, 495 and Bonesteel, *Henry Darger*, 11.

17 MacGregor, *In the Realms of the Unreal*, footnotes, Chapter 3, no. 40.

18 For example, Darger writes in his journal: "Almost about to throw the ball (of twine) at Christ statue. Blame me for my bad luck in things, I'm sorry to say so. I'll always be this way, always was and I don't give a damn." Darger, *History of My Life*, dated Saturday, April 7, 1968.

19 MacGregor, *In the Realms of the Unreal*, footnotes, Chapter 3, no. 40.

20 Due to its damaged appearance, MacGregor suggests that the Vivian collage may be the same "child pictures" that withstood Darger's violent outburst. MacGregor, *In the Realms of the Unreal*, 147.

21 St. Thérèse often elicits both admiration and loathing for her childish obedience and incessant desire for sainthood. One biographer, Vita Sackville-West described her manner as *niaiserie*, or "sugariness." Another biographer, Monica Furlong, refers to her own fascination with the Little Flower as "embarrassing." See Vita Sackville-West, *The Eagle and the Dove* (London: Michael Joseph, 1943) and Monica Furlong, *Thérèse of Lisieux* (London: Virago Press, 1987).

22 Mary Frohlich, *St. Thérèse of Lisieux: Essential Writings* (Maryknoll, NY: Orbis Books, 2003), 34–35.

23 John Saward, *The Way of the Lamb: The Spirit of Childhood and the End of the Age* (San Francisco, CA: Ignatius Press, 1999), 27.

24 Saward posits that the *Little Way* is a guide to applying the state of baptismal grace, rebirth by water and the Holy Spirit as a child of God, to everyday life. Adult sins strip away this state while Sacraments rejuvenate spiritual childhood. See Saward, *The Way of the Lamb*, 28–30.

25 Matthew 18:3–4.

26 The 1932 newsletter, "Society of the Little Flower and the Confraternity of the Scapular Carmelite Monastery" was published by the society's national headquarters in Chicago, IL. It is part of the Henry Darger Room Collection and Archives at Intuit: The Center for Intuitive and Outsider Art, Chicago. The 1959 monthly newsletter titled, *The Little Flower* was published by the Discalced Carmelite Fathers in Oklahoma City, OK. This piece of ephemera and a standard holy card bearing an image of the saint are part of the Henry Darger Papers at the American Folk Art Museum Library and Archives, New York (Box 73, Files 13 and 17). The repurposed letters are noted in Mary Trent's research concerning Darger's fabrication of letters for his fictional Children's Protective Society certificates. Trent argues that these letters indicate Darger's participation in Catholic charities, specifically one devoted to the Little Flower of Christ. See Mary Trent, "Many Stirring Scenes," 91–92.

27 Quoted in Saward, *The Way of the Lamb*, 77. During Pope Pius X's short tenure (1903–1914) he reinstated communion to children as young as seven and beatified Joan of Arc (1909).

28 Song of Solomon 4:12.

29 See the entry for "violet" in Jennifer Speake, *The Dent Dictionary of Symbols in Christian Art* (London: J.M. Dent, 1994), 151. According to legend, wild violets carpet the nearly desolate site of Montserrat near Barcelona where the faithful come to worship the Virgin Mary. Pilgrims acknowledge the violets as a physical sign and mystic message of Mary's power over fertility. Marina Warner, *Alone of All Her Sex: The Myth and Cult of the Virgin Mary* (New York: Vintage Books, 1983), 273.

30 Floral names were a popular choice for girls throughout the nineteenth century and into the twentieth. Nineteenth-century literature, from Thorstein Veblen's *Theory of the Leisure Class* (1899) to ladies' magazines and advice manuals associated femininity—assumed as socially passive, dependent, and ornamental—with the nature of flowers. For an extensive history of floral symbolism see Beverly Seaton, *The Language of Flowers: A History* (Charlottesville: University Press of Virginia, 1995). See the entry for "daisy" in George Ferguson,

Signs and Symbols in Christian Art (New York: Oxford University Press, 1955), 36. Also, the English Daisy, which closes at night was known in Victorian times as the flower of children and innocence. "Daisy," The Columbia Encyclopedia, sixth edition, Columbia University Press, accessed April 3, 2006, www.bartleby.com/65/da/daisy.html.

31 Darger, *In the Realms of the Unreal*, Volume 11, 463.

32 From Darger's poem "The Mexican's Song" quoted in Bonesteel, *Henry Darger*, 50.

33 Like the fictional "Miss Virgie," Daisy Low was also a daughter of a Confederate officer.

34 See the Harvard University Open Library Collections Program for an online version of 1913 Girl Scouts Manual: Juliette Gordon Low, "How Girls Can Help Their Country," *Open Collections Program, Harvard University Libraries*, accessed June 12, 2006, http://pds.harvard.edu:8080/pdx/servlet/pds?

35 Only two other girls in this composition wear similar pansy skirts. They stand at either end.

36 In Victorian symbolism, the pansy represents the memory of friends evoking the face of loved ones as if a miniature portrait. See Susan Stewart, *On Longing: Narratives of the Miniature, the Gigantic, the Souvenir, the Collection* (Durham: Duke University Press, 1993), 41.

37 See Seaton, *The Language of Flowers*, 176–177 for the iconography of the pansy.

38 Darger, *In the Realms of the Unreal*, Volume XII, 202a–202b, also numbered 2484–2485. MacGregor notes that this passage is under a section entitled, "Were Violet and her sisters rewarded for their patient suffering for our Lord and Savior Jesus Christ?"

39 Frohlich, *St. Thérèse of Lisieux*, 64–65.

40 Joan of Arc is another gender-bending female saint and exemplar to the Vivians represented in Darger's *In the Realms of the Unreal*. Her role in Darger's story is discussed in the following chapter.

41 See Warner's full discussion of Joan's name in "Maid of France" from Marina Warner, *Joan of Arc: The Image of Female Heroism* (Berkeley: University of California Press, 1999), 13–31.

42 Medieval scholar Jocelyn Wogan-Browne concurs, citing vernacular usage distinguishing virgin from *pucelle* and maiden as internalized and graded hierarchical states of virginity. See Jocelyn Wogan-Browne, "Chaste Bodies: Frames and Experiences," in *Framing Medieval Bodies*, edited by Sarah Kay and Miri Rubin (Manchester: Manchester University Press, 1994), 26.

43 The Little Flower, a devotee to Joan of Arc, penned two plays about the warrior maiden's life and spiritual calling.

44 The calyx is an outer whorl of tiny leaves that protects the inner bud. Most calyxes bear a green color except for the lily, passion flower, and orchid. In regards to these three flowers, scientists believe that their colorful calyxes help to attract pollinators.

45 Frohlich, *St. Thérèse of Lisieux*, 66.

46 Ibid, 67.

47 Karen Winstead and Margaret Miles provide thorough backgrounds on the narrative conventions of Catholic virgin martyrs. See Winstead's introduction, "Generic Virgin Martyr," in *Virgin Martyrs: Legends of Sainthood in Late*

Medieval England (Ithaca: Cornell University Press, 1997), 5–18 and Margaret Miles, *Carnal Knowing: Female Nakedness and Religious Meaning in the Christian West* (Boston: Beacon Press, 1989), 53–77.

48 "The best virgin, it seems, is always a dead virgin," according to Medieval scholar Jocelyn Wogan-Browne. In Catholic lore, these heroines of chastity long to be tortured, dismembered, and eventually killed in a glorious and loyal passion for Christ. See Wogan-Browne, "Chaste Bodies," 24.

49 Darger, *In the Realms of the Unreal*, Volume IV, 380.

50 Cited in Bonesteel, *Henry Darger*, 130, as a handwritten draft in Darger's journal.

51 Other girls like Annie Aronburg or Jennie Turmer visually blend in with the Vivians. They, as all girls in Darger's vision, become martyrs for the Christian cause.

52 Proverbs 9:4.

53 Examples of wartime adventures for girls include "Dora Darling, the Daughter of the Regiment" by Jane Goodwin Austin and *The Boys and Girls Stories of the War* containing "Helen Norcross, or the Two Friends." See Alice Fahs, "A Boys' and Girls' War," in *The Imagined Civil War: Popular Literature of the North & South, 1861–1865* (Chapel Hill: The University of North Carolina Press, 2001), 256–286.

54 Little Nell, a model of self-sacrifice in Dickens's *Old Curiosity Shop*, leaves the city with her grandfather to escape urban evils. She falls mysteriously ill and dies. Quoted in Frank Donovan, *The Children of Charles Dickens* (London: Leslie Frewin, 1969), 102.

55 Darger, *In the Realms of the Unreal*, Volume I, 17.

56 Although a copy of *Uncle Tom's Cabin* was not found in Darger's apartment, it appears that he had one in his possession at some time due to his extensive use of Stowe's words and characters. Little Eva continually serves as a measuring device for suffering in Darger's writings: "hundreds of sad incidents like Little Eva in 'Uncle Tom's Cabin' occurred." Darger, *In the Realms of the Unreal*, Volume III, 530.

57 The most blatant appropriation of Stowe's novel involves the third and fourth paragraphs of her Preface:

"The poet, the painter, and the artist now seek out and embellish the common and gentler humanities of life, and, under the allurements of fiction, breathe a humanizing and subduing influence, favorable to the development of the great principles of Christian brotherhood.

The hand of benevolence is everywhere stretched out, searching into abuses, righting wrongs, alleviating distresses, and bringing to the knowledge and sympathies of the world the lowly, the oppressed, and the forgotten."

Darger's variation reads:

"The poet, the painter and the artist, even if they were to seek this all out under the allurement of fiction or truth, could not have accomplished more.

As is observed here, the desolation of the war in every incomprehensible way is everywhere stretched out, roaring into abuses of child slaves, increasing wicked wrongs, redoubling distresses, and bringing the attention of the world to the horrors of disasters that were never heard of in real experiences and history, thus bringing the sympathies of the world to the lowly child slaves, and Abbieannia's cause."

Harriet Beecher Stowe, *Preface* of *Uncle Tom's Cabin, or Life among the Lowly* (New York: Bantam Books, 1981 ed. 1851–52), xvii; Darger, *In the Realms of the Unreal*, Volume III, unnumbered first page.

58 Stowe, *Preface* of *Uncle Tom's Cabin*, 406; Cited in MacGregor, *In the Realms of the Unreal*, 274 from Darger's reference journal, 429.

59 Stowe, *Preface* of *Uncle Tom's Cabin*, 166.

60 Similarly, Marina Warner argues that Joan of Arc's legendary amenorrhea underscores her state of purity and denies clear sexual identification of her body with the adult female world. Warner, *Joan of Arc*, 139–158.

61 Darger, *In the Realms of the Unreal*, Volume I, 122.

62 Stowe, *Preface* of *Uncle Tom's Cabin*, 335 and 337.

63 Darger, *In the Realms of the Unreal*, Volume 3, 823.

64 Ibid, 829.

65 Stewart, *On Longing*, 44.

66 St. Thérèse was four years old when her mother died. "Papa" was her nickname for God. Frohlich, *St. Thérèse of Lisieux*, 52.

67 Stowe, *Preface* of *Uncle Tom's Cabin*, 313.

68 See MacGregor, "Thoughts on the Question: Why Darger?," *The Outsider* 2:2 (Winter 1998): 15 and MacGregor, *In the Realms of the Unreal*, 23.

2   Girls on the Run[1]

On an envelope containing photographic negatives, Henry Darger wrote, "little girl on the run, maybe draw in massacre picture."[2] Like so many other notations on carbon paper, scrapbook pages, and bits of random ephemera, this label served a dual purpose of directing the artist's attention to content as well as to potential use. The negatives, sourced from his local drugstore, signify an important development in Darger's artistic practices; that is, through photographic enlargement, he found a means to enhance the scale of figurative elements, while retaining their proportional integrity. Unsure of his ability to draw, Darger rendered form through copying and tracing, occasionally adding collaged elements and small penciled in additions. Photographic enlargement, traced by his own hand, allowed him to create modifications in scale and dramatic, perspectival arrangements. Art historians cite and celebrate this development among others, as evidence of Darger's ingenuity.[3] Additionally, in an *oeuvre* that is notoriously difficult to date accurately, the stamped drugstore receipts within enlargement envelopes establish a ballpark commencement date (post-1944) for later components of Darger's work.

Often overlooked, however, is the significance of the "little girl on the run" motif and the artist's predetermination of her placement in "massacre pictures." One finds this sprinter, a haunting and powerful liminal figure, in dangerous, action-packed scenarios where waves of girls run, fight, or bravely stand their ground. Within "massacre pictures"—representations of seemingly arbitrary child-butchery and ritualistic martyrdoms, as well as predatory natural occurrences—approaching storms, fires, and tornadoes—the little girl on the run becomes the dominant motif traveling the infinite terrain of Darger's war-torn epic.

Within the imagery for *In the Realms of the Unreal*, the running girl reads as more than just an image of flight, rather she lingers in Darger's drawings as a mercurial emblem of mobility, (re)combination, playfulness, and social transgression. Darger frequently elects to depict the running girl naked or partially clothed, further exposing her little body to potential harm.[4] Her vulnerable, open, and active state permits Darger to selectively add hand-drawn, schematic male genitalia between parting and extending little legs. With a few, simple pencil marks, Darger fabricates a complex, fantastic intersex[5] child—a queer figure of motility and fluid mutability (Figure 2.1). Her visage becomes a blur of both motion and sex. Ever expansive, as she morphs back and forth between little girl and epicene creation, she additionally embodies metaphysical proportions. Throughout his narrative, Darger associates his fictional children with martyrdom, and thus, witnessing: "Holy Innocents," he said, "who would be terrible witnesses against all things recorded against the Glandelinians. . . ."[6] Her significant form,

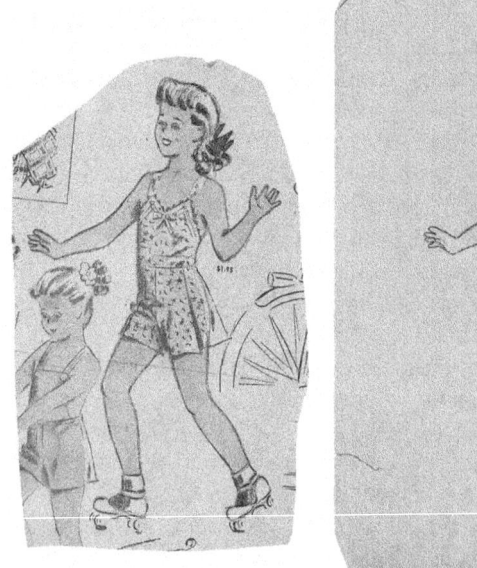
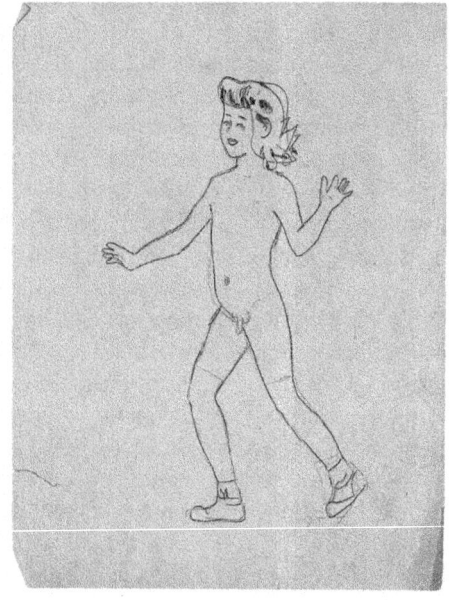

Figure 2.1 Henry Darger (1892–1973) © ARS, NY. Untitled (fashion illustration and tracing), mid-twentieth century. Newspaper illustration with pencil markings (left); carbon tracing with pencil on paper (right) 24.13 × 13.97 cm (left); 27.94 × 21.59 cm (right). Gift of Kiyoko Lerner, 2003.7.13A, B

sacred, yet, profanely rendered naked and sexually indeterminate simultaneously reinforces and troubles her little girl sainthood.

Indeed, visible signs of ambiguously gendered, sexed childhood run throughout the lush landscapes of Darger's art. Curiously, the artist himself does not explain, or even mention, intersex bodies or sexual hybridity in his voluminous detailed narrative and captions for visual works. His prose, instead, insists upon the beauty, purity, and wholesome integrity of the seven Vivians and the thousands of little girls populating his tale. Consider, for example, this belabored passage in which Darger describes his ultimate girl crusaders:

> Whatever else was beautiful or dainty or delightful faded to nothingness when contrasted with the bewitching faces of the Vivian Girls, and it has often been said by those who know that no other ruler in all the world, nor any children, boys or girls or even women, can ever hope to equal, or ever will equal or even get anywhere near to it, the gracious charm of their manner, loveliness, and righteousness that equaled their features.[7]

Furthermore, his imagery provides no indication that anatomical differences disrupt these aesthetic and moral traits, or that bodies with intersex characteristics equate in any manner to corruption, sin, or vice. In any given scenario, Vivians and other girl protagonists may reveal or not show any signs of these differences. If intersex characteristics are a kind of metamorphosis or instantaneous change, it conforms to the Vivian naturally—without need for explanation or great spectacle in itself.[8] Given the frequency of such transformative situations and the important role it plays in representing the sacred girl body, one must assume that this fluid morphology signifies meaning, aligning with Vivian traits of purity and virtue. Nevertheless, Darger's penciled in additions literally draw attention to sexual organs and, for some scholars, erotically charge the little girl body.

As such, this transgressive "girl" rendered a psychoanalytic and sometimes puerile reading in the majority of early Darger scholarship, precluding other interpretations. One of the most prominent scholars, John M. MacGregor leads this line of thought, arguing that the artist is caught between "knowing and not knowing" in regards to the physical differences between boys and girls.[9] MacGregor infantilizes Darger, claiming that his understanding of sex and sexuality is stunted and in many ways a form of innocence. Relying on the theory of Freudian castration anxiety, MacGregor sums up the image of the epicene child in Darger's art as the result of sexual regression into infantile complexes, yet he additionally hints at adult sexual perversion with, "other possibilities . . . too frightening to contemplate."[10] MacGregor's psychoanalytic approach treats Darger's representations of children as diagnostic material and thus reduces the imagery to a manifestation of the artist's disturbed psyche.[11]

Although the study by MacGregor remains the most informative text on Darger's art and life, scholarly interest in relying on psycho-biographical methods has waned in recent years in favor of research that considers cultural influences in tandem with the artist's material resources and other methodologies. Shortly before MacGregor's study was published, writer and curator, Michael Bonesteel pioneered this new direction with brief, yet significant observations relating to Darger's collections of newspaper clippings and children's literature. Bonesteel raised questions regarding the artist's intentionality in rendering sexual dualism. Specifically, he wondered if this girl equipped with male genitalia could be an attempt to indicate a mythological state, a child body endowed with a "warrior status."[12] Bonesteel noted that like St. Joan of Arc, the Vivian Girls exhibit a kind of supernatural quality aligning with their mutual cross-dressing and military prowess. Later, in a 2009 MoMA catalogue, Klaus Biesenbach suggested that Darger's variant child shares a kinship with a character from L. Frank Baum's second Oz series, *The Marvellous Land of Oz* (1904).[13] In this sequel to *The Wonderful Wizard of Oz* (1900), the boy-protagonist Tip learns that he was once the Princess Ozma, transformed through a magical spell cast by the witch Mombi. After pressure from the Sorceress Glinda, Mombi agrees to change Tip back to his previous sex and identity, so that he can begin his/her reign as the princess. Darger owned first editions of the complete *The Wonderful Wizard of Oz* and its thirteen sequels and incorporated Oz characters and locations into his own, *In the Realms of the Unreal*. Although Tip is not specifically incorporated in Darger's tale, Biesenbach proposes that a sense of fairy tale enchantment, appropriated from the Oz series, plays a significant role in Darger's representations of sexually mutable bodies.

Michael Moon's recent publication, *Darger's Resources*, presents the most significant departure from dominant pathologizing interpretations of Darger's depictions of little girls. Comparing Darger's "sequelating" literary energies to those of early twentieth-century comic strips, illustrated children's adventure stories, war chronicles, and pulp magazines, Moon asserts that such popular and relatively inexpensive literary sources provided more than aesthetic models for Darger; they also offered intellectual fodder.[14] Extending his discussion to Catholic virgin-martyr narratives, Moon draws connections between the violence inflicted upon Darger's girl martyrs and stories of the acts of female martyrs venerated before the reforms of the Second Vatican Council (1962–1965). While Moon doesn't directly address the image of the child with intersex characteristics, his conclusions establish a point of departure important to this chapter. Moon argues that in spite of being socially isolated, Darger was "a product of the devotional and spiritual tendencies of the Roman Catholic Church."[15] Moreover, he contends that Darger's creative output should be examined against, not outside of, mainstream culture. "His world," says Moon,

> was not really a private or secret one, particular or unique to him (no matter how clandestine his characteristic mode of working may have been), as much as it was in many ways a public one composed of the myriad elements scavenged during a lifetime of reading and viewing and collecting images and narratives and rhetorics from a bewildering array of sources.[16]

By investigating the fluid transmissions between the spaces of artistic production, popular culture, and religious veneration, this chapter questions the reduction of Darger's art, specifically his little girl imagery, to pathologic production and psycho-biographical explanation. Accordingly, this essay builds upon the momentum of recent scholarship that contextualizes Darger's art within secular and religious cultural spheres by examining relationships between Vivian Girls and so-called, "virile" female saints celebrated in Catholic devotional cults. His appropriation and use of holy cards, martyr narratives, as well as his own variations on specific martyrs' names and their legendary, fluid gender suggest a divine lineage between the Vivians and female martyrs like SS. Vivia Perpetua and Joan of Arc. Specifically, this connection lies within narrative tropes retelling their hagiography in which "becoming male" marks the transcendence of gendered differences and thus, access to holiness. Pursuing these connections, the following line of inquiry opens the possibilities for further discussion of Darger's Vivians within a broad-ranging, less eroticized framework, by bringing this girl into the context of art and religion. Her precocious, contradictorily sexed body and indeterminate gender speak broadly, and with rich complexity, to belief structures concerning the role of the transgressive female body within the Catholic faith as a potent sign of piety. As importantly, her changeling form illustrates the artist's desire to fabricate an extraordinary child beyond nature—capable both of defeating bloodthirsty Glandelinians and rebelling against conventional girlhood. As such, I argue that Darger's girl with intersex characteristics does not culminate in a denial of difference—a succinct conclusion determining the artist's sexual perversion. Instead, she remains a multivalent symbolic force sprinting through fantastical possibilities and orienting toward other symbolic texts (here, female saints). The running, girl-in-motion is a sacred image verging on sacrilege, a slippage between gendered/sexed polarities of female and male—super-fluid and spilling all over the place.

A Typical Scenario: Little Girls on the Run

In *AT SUNBEAM CREEK . . . At Torrington* (Figure 2.2), the Vivian Girl operates on pure *vivam* (literally, "I shall live"), evading impending doom and awaiting her next surge of energy. A tripartite construction, each scene appears as a distinct cell with the capacity of telling individual stories. Although these three scenes jump from bright day to black forest to blazing firestorm, they flow together under the narrative aegis of a thrilling chase— one in which a predatory fire endangers the lives of little girls.

The heat in this final passage palpitates. A wall of bright yellow flames with slight orange modeling and rising, faint striations covers the top half of the image. Flaming debris falls from the sky. The glare of the fire is equally matched by the conspicuous disrobing of the girls—one without a blouse, two bearing shoulders, and four with only tattered pieces hanging from their upper torsos. This latter group, almost completely naked, display schematic penises. These figures elevate the climactic moment of this scene through surprise and sudden revelation of their sexually mutable bodies.

Captions from this fiery triad offer little, if any, clues to the mysterious, transformative finale. Darger's notations follow a chase narrative, fixating

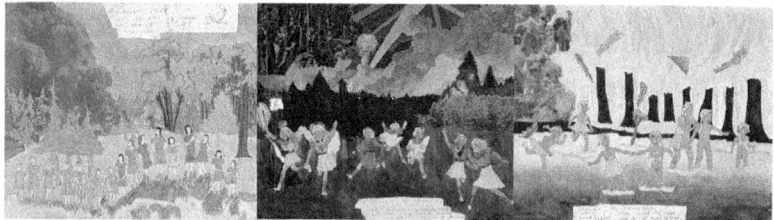

Figure 2.2 Henry Darger (1892–1973) © ARS, NY. AT SUNBEAM CREEK. Are with little girl refugees again in peril from forest fires, but escape this also, but half naked and in burned rags/At Torrington. Are persued (sic) by a storm of fire but save themselves by jumping into a stream and swim across as seen in the next picture/At Torrington. They reach the river just in the nick of time. Their red color is caused by the glare of flames. . . (double-sided), mid-twentieth century. Watercolor, pencil, carbon tracing, and collage on pieced paper 19 × 70 ½". Anonymous gift in recognition of Sam Farber © Kiyoko Lerner 2004.1.2A

Source: Photo: James Prinz. American Folk Art Museum, New York, NY, U.S.A. Photo credit: American Folk Art Museum/Art Resource, NY © 2020 Kiyoko Lerner/Artists Rights Society (ARS), New York

on the last image. The episode begins with the first caption: "At Sunbeam Creek. Are with little girl refugees again in peril from forest fires. But escape this also, but half naked and in burned rags."[17] Curiously, this caption does not narrate the companion scene. Darger's yearning to arrive at the last inflamed passage surfaces again in the second panel: "At Torrington. Are persued (sic) by a storm of fire but save themselves by jumping into a stream and swim across as seen in the next picture."[18] Here, again, instead of attending to the immediate image, Darger impatiently pushes on to the final scene. Once there, he reticently divulges what appears before our eyes: "Their red color is caused by glare of flames. At Torrington. They reach the river just in the nick of time."[19] Without warning, Darger leaps beyond his captions and the societal norms of physiology by visually transforming the little girl body. Revealing her form's recombination, Darger moves this child, already in motion, beyond the category of "girl" into something transgressively unique. She emerges triumphant in the last panel, playing, dancing and unaffected by her nakedness.

Re-envisioning Gender and "Nuded" Children

Little girl refugees, wearing next to nothing, flee the firestorm in *AT SUNBEAM CREEK . . . At Torrington*. Naked girls aim and fire rifles (some still in their Mary Jane shoes, anklet socks, and wide-brim hats) in *six episodes, three places not mentioned. Escape during violent storm, still fighting though persued (sic) for long distance*[20] and another naked group sprints across a panoramic expanse in *At Jennie Richee. Assuming nuded appearance by compulsion race ahead of coming storm to warn their father.*[21] In these action-packed scenes, and countless others, nakedness conveys multiple and contradictory messages of strength and vigor, bravery, innocence, and powerlessness. Referring to Darger's girls as "naked" reflects my own thoughts (and projection) onto his unclothed or partially clothed children. I use the term to suggest a state of transition and exposure, deprived of clothing and vulnerable. Darger describes his girls as both "naked" and "nude," often preferring the term "nuded."[22] Darger's nuded girls denote a passive context indicating that somehow, forces (known or unknown) strip girls of their clothing. Nuded happens, and as Darger's art attests, the girls do not mind, except, of course, when fiery tongues of flame or Glandelinian hands disrobe them. Girls frolic in fields, battle foes, and run for the hills in various states of undress. Darger shows them forgoing gestures of modesty, expressing, instead, an Edenic shamelessness and athletic prowess, comfortable and quite capable of multiple and dangerous tasks, *nuded*.

By creating his own term for the girls' disrobed condition, Darger suggests a third state—neither this nor that—signaling something unrestrained and in-between.[23] Such liminality, a moment of escape from biological and socially constructed boundaries, allows his protagonists to exist, however briefly, within a transgressive and possibly transcendent form. Simultaneously, the girls also evade certain death—a renowned Vivian skill. Etymologically speaking, the morphing "Vivian" denotes her perpetual will to live . . . "Vivam!" Much like a super hero, she is still alive and transformed.

Comparison of an original drawing of a girl from the Sears Roebuck catalogue with Darger's traced variation (Figure 2.1) illustrates the way in which he extruded "nuded" children from representations of girls that populated mass culture's advertisements, coloring books, and comic strips. This example, a girl in a short jumper and roller skates, translates onto the carbon paper as a nearly nude girl with intersex characteristics, wearing only socks and shoes. Darger pulls a pencil along the silhouette of her diminutive figure, imagining her form beneath the folds of cloth. Schematic male genitalia complete her open-legged, active pose. Drawing becomes for Darger an act of penetrating scrutiny; he disrobes the girl in order to know what lies behind the surface of her exterior. The act of tracing—both of re-enactment and creation—allowed Darger, beginning with a girl's essential form, to imaginatively unlock secrets of Vivian girlhood that are latent in images from popular culture. Drawing instigated a literal exposure, a frank revealing of the openness and ambiguous potential of girl bodies. By creating a *nuded* form, Darger reclaimed her "innocent" and "natural" origins while simultaneously re-inventing the girl by re-inscribing and re-combining her palimpsest body into a child of remarkable powers, beauty, and wonder.

Ephemera collected and traced by the artist, such as coloring book imagery and *Parents Magazine* articles about the newest little girl fashions, signal that Darger was keenly aware of society's determination of girlish femininity and its commercial trappings. He replicated the petticoats, braided ponytails, and Mary Jane shoes comprising attire for girls ages 7–12 and dressed the denizens of the *In the Realms of the Unreal* in the codes and conventions of the day that outwardly announced their age-appropriate femininity. Multiple traced details on paper of hairstyles, shoes, and attire reveal Darger's interest in getting this gendered minutia "right." However, in his prose, Darger associates biological sex predominately through hairstyle and hair length. Bouncy curls and flowing locks signify "female." Short-cropped hair signifies "male." Passages in his narrative confirm this pattern:

[S]he (Jennie Turmer) was adapting to her slender and pretty little form a little boy's attire, in which it was deemed safest she should make her escape to the Christian army, under the Emperor.

'Now for the needed sacrifice,' said she as she stood before a looking glass, and shook down her silky abundance of golden curly hair. . . . Jennie turned to the glass, and the scissors glittered as one long lock after another was detached so that she wore now short bobbed hair.[24]

A masquerade of male gender implicitly informs this passage. Declaring herself a pretty boy, Jennie admires her own transcendent beauty and blushes as she takes her performance further by flirting with Angelinia. A few paragraphs later, Jennie and her compatriots discuss boyish mannerisms:

'And I must stamp and take long steps like a boy, and look saucy.' 'Don't exert yourself too much on that.' said Gertrude. 'There is now and then sissy young boys who act like girls you know, and I think therefore it would be better and easier to act like a boy who is in the class of sissies.'[25]

Acting like a boy who acts like a girl, Jennie sets out on her escape. We learn here that boys exhibit a vigorous gait and, perhaps of consequence to Darger's depictions of lunging and running children with intersex characteristics, "take long steps." In this imaginary world, gender and sex[26] twist and turn on the child's body as a tool for adaptation. These slippages prove valuable, even necessary for saving the day. Darger visualizes his warrior child (the fantasy Jennie) resplendent with cross-identifications of girlhood and boyhood.

Accordingly, in *In the Realms of the Unreal*, hair prevails as a signifier of gender while genital differences carry less specificity in determining girls from boys. Moreover, the sex of characters in Darger's world appears to be unconnected to primary or secondary sexual characteristics, and instead displaced on other markers (like hair and patterns of movement). The few boys that do appear in his art maintain their short hairstyle and genital designations. Little girls, on the other hand, possess loose, mutable forms. Girl bodies with both girlish hairstyles and male genitals never fully morph into boys. Gendered hair traits remain, even in this in-between state. Captions accompanying such unique images, like *AT SUNBEAM CREEK . . . At Torrington*, continue to assert that we "Are with *Little Girl* Refugees Again." While his written words do not speak of an obvious transformation, Darger's verbose imagery indicates that these in-between protagonists fluctuate between girl and "girlish," exhibiting a sense of continuance—a becoming—without a final transformative endpoint.

In addition to denuding his figures, Darger also gleaned some of his illustrations of unclothed children directly from material culture. A small portion of his magazine and newspaper clippings feature children in the nude and partial dress. Found newspaper photographs, such as one displaying prepubescent girls informally posing in a bathtub[27] and another of nude children dancing in a circle with an accompanying caption, "Back to Nature Play"[28] may have served as figure studies and even confirmation from mainstream culture that child nudity equates with an innocent, care-free state. Furthermore, these images frequently offer visual comparisons between little girls and boys where sexual difference is ambiguous. Three girls and a boy are strikingly similar in one newspaper photograph saved by Darger (Figure 2.3). Shirtless and in what appears to be white underwear, this foursome sits on a bench and quietly observes something or someone

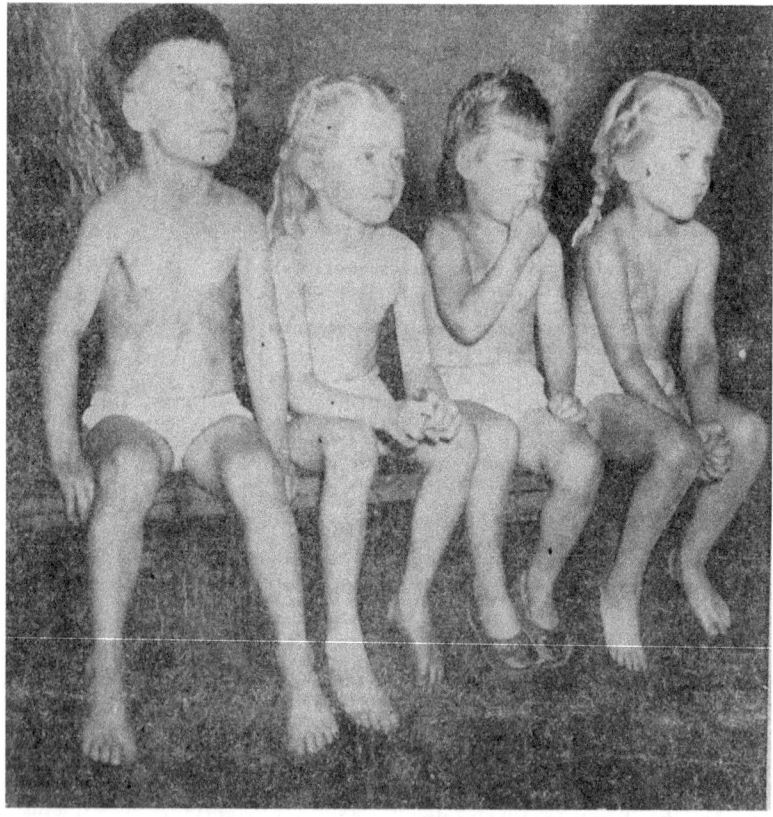

Figure 2.3 Henry Darger (1892–1973) © ARS, NY. Newspaper Photograph of four children in bench. Henry Darger Papers, Box 95, Folder 16. American Folk Art Museum, New York, NY, U.S.A.

Source: Photo credit: American Folk Art Museum/Art Resource, NY © 2020 Kiyoko Lerner/ Artists Rights Society (ARS), New York

outside the picture. Due to their prepubescent age, their bodies share simi-
larities in shape. The boy, however, displays a slightly larger frame. Only
long braided hair on the girls distinguish their noticeable difference from
the boy. Although this clipped newspaper image does not contain a date or
name of source, it seems probable that it was taken from a local Chicago
newspaper in the mid-1950s–1960s along with numerous, other variations
of girls and boys, partially dressed.[29] At times, these images include short,
charming narratives further emphasizing how ordinary it may have been to
see little children partially undressed in the newspaper. One such example
is, "Little Debbie Compton," a shirtless 3-year-old, who gives the camera
an impish smile as we learn she was "chasing fire trucks" in the middle
of the night and rescued by Detroit police who "warmed her up with hot
chocolate."[30]

While some scholars refer to this collection of clippings as Darger's
"private erotica,"[31] I wish to point out that these images originate from
"legitimate" and public sources—*Ladies Home Journal, Life Magazine*,
and various Chicago newspapers. If anything, these images of children are
our erotica. At the risk of positioning Darger as a passive victim caught
up within a lurid cultural phenomenon, I argue that this type of imagery,
intended to confer "innocence," in either nudity or partial undress was
plentiful in American mass media of the early to mid-twentieth century.
Our current-day reaction to this resource material is informed by our
twenty-first-century fears. I will admit that Darger's attachment to these
images exceeds what one considers ordinary and that we do not fully know
why the artist collected these images. However, "ordinary," like "normal,"
is a relative term tied to a culturally specific consensus of ideas, and Darger
did very little, if anything, within "ordinary" limits or in moderation. He
sought these photos and advertisements out, compiling multiples on certain themes. Some were modified and used as templates for girls in *In the
Realms of the Unreal*. For example, he acquired seventeen copies of the
Coppertone Girl[32] using her form to create a surprised child that looks over
her left shoulder, as in *[Storm] brewing. This is not a strawberry the little
girl is carrying. It comes from a paradise tree . . .*[33]

Theorist James Kincaid argues that, for adults, images of children produce both uneasiness and joy: "the child carries for us things we somehow
cannot carry ourselves, sometimes anxieties we want to be divorced from
and sometimes pleasures so great we would not without the child, know
how to contain them."[34] Kincaid's scholarship offers a cultural context for
analyzing Darger's art. His examination of Victorian literature encompasses
sentimentalized depictions of childhood familiar to Darger—for instance,
characters by J.M. Barrie, Lewis Carroll, Charles Dickens, and Harriet
Beecher Stowe. Likewise, Kincaid's investigations into the eroticization

of innocence extend into American twentieth-century narratives of child abduction, the phenomenon of child movie stars, and advertising imagery. Again, his subjects align with mainstream concerns, interests, and visual resources that are relevant to Darger's art and writings. Kincaid asserts that American culture strives to protect and preserve images of childhood, associating children with innocence and with a carefree and pre-sexual state. Darger's art complicates these associations. However, Kincaid suggests, culture also complicates images of children. He persuasively argues that the child, pure and stainless, acts as a foil for our disavowed desires. As America's iconic treatment of the Coppertone Girl advertisement implies, culture cultivates this movement between sexuality and non-sexual innocence, further eroticizing the child. Kincaid warns that our culture dwells on this image, and other child-manifestations with "underpants on the way off," for the wrong reasons: "Not only do we read our adult desires back onto the blushing child, there's a crude allegory of cultural practice here as well, an emblem of vigorous duplicity: we uncover what we shield, censure what we enjoy."[35]

American culture's slippages of innocence and sexuality create, eroticize, and commodify the Coppertone Girl and numerous other girl-figures (in uniforms, frilly dresses, and Mary Jane shoes). These girls come to Darger's art ready-made, overflowing with (veiled but embodied) erotic potential and emotional investment. So, if we are to believe Kincaid, then the art world eroticizes Darger's girls as much as the artist does—perhaps more. Cultural constructs of sexual fantasy and repressed paranoia create interest in, and concern for, this aspect of Darger's work. Speaking of Darger's imagery as contained within *his* pathologic fetish further disavows the fact that Darger's work participates in a larger cultural phenomenon of uncovering and shielding the child.[36]

If we can, for a moment, set aside the psychoanalytic notion that the nude image of a child with intersex characteristics is a product of Darger's own peculiarly skewed reality and consider instead that we are dealing with a representation, or more accurately, a complex pastiche with multivalent meanings, we begin to plumb the depths of the image's potential. However, like all else in *In the Realms of the Unreal*, no singular rule or code regulates representation. One type in Darger's repertoire sharply contrasts the active, defiant child sprinting through action-packed scenes. I describe her here as a "girl-with-pail" figure, often depicted by Darger as upright, frontally displaying her *nuded* form and schematic male genitalia.[37] Sometimes with a finger to her mouth, and/or a tucked arm behind her back, this recurring child-motif subtly projects her body forward toward the viewer. Her defining cuteness, a coy plea for attention, manifests in her upturned eyes and tucked-in chin. The pail that she holds doubles as a signifier of her playful nature and her toil as slave. Inert, she appears to play the willing victim—another variation of the "martyr" in Darger's visual art.

The Vivian Girl, a visual template for the thousands of little girls in the artist's work, procures vitality and significance through flux, an excessive metamorphosis comprising transgressive boundary crossings and the surprise encounters of incongruous elements. Throughout Darger's *In the Realms of the Unreal*, female bodies are transformed and empowered within an anatomical and gendered spectrum. They share this trait in common with female Catholic saints, especially those renowned for their virile nature and gender-bending appearance.

Female Saints "Becoming Male"

Darger's Catholic faith permeated every aspect of his life. He grew up in Catholic boys homes, worked in Catholic hospitals, covered his apartment with holy cards, iconic statuettes, crucifixes, and chromolithographs, and went to Mass daily, often making multiple trips for novenas and feast days. He died in a Catholic nursing home. With a self-deprecating humor, he referred to himself as a "sorry saint"[38] while he created a vast, imaginary world teeming with soldiers of Catholic nations fighting for the release of little girls enslaved by godless foes.

Many elements of Catholic material culture remain obvious and identifiable in Darger's art (e.g., traced and collaged holy cards and Sacred Heart images).[39] However, his visual re-conception of a mutable, and as I argue, thus symbolically holy female body, presents us with a hybrid creation difficult to categorize, let alone pinpoint to a single devotional image. Turning to the wealth of fantastic stories within Catholic literature describing physical transformations, as well as belief structures blurring gendered boundaries, provides us with a strong corollary to Darger's equally supernatural Vivian Girl. Suffering for the Christian cause, his little girls, like Catholic female martyrs and mystics, display astounding self-control and physical strength. The little girls additionally demonstrate their Christ-like fortitude through their gender-bending, mutable bodies during intense moments that test their resolve.

By "becoming male," or performing "maleness," certain female saints rebuked social and biological determinations of roles. According to theologian Margaret Miles, such "male" performances included: practicing forms of asceticism (maintenance of chastity and virginity, fasting), estranging themselves from patriarchal figures and domesticity, changing bodily appearance, and exhibiting spiritual fortitude.[40] Male hagiographers described these "virile" women as "more like men than nature would seem to allow."[41]

Examples from this "male" genre include Thecla, a beautiful noblewoman who repudiates her engagement to retain her virginity, alienates her family, and follows the Apostle Paul. Thecla cut her hair and wore men's clothes in order to travel freely and avoid rape. Pelagia masqueraded as a man and joined a monastery (her gender was discovered after her death). The fictitious St. Uncumber, or St. Wilgefortis, a ten-year-old girl, popular in the Roman Catholic Church from the fifteenth century through the liturgical reform of Vatican II, was crucified by her father for magically sprouting a beard the night before her arranged marriage. Usually represented nailed to a cross, this bearded woman is often confused with a crucified Christ. Wilgefortis is derived from *virgo fortis* (or strong virgin). This saint was also known as *Libertata* and *Librada* (liberty) in Italy and Spain, respectively.[42] Even if not currently sanctified by the Catholic Church, the stories of these women, and many others, survive through tales told to young girls at Catholic Schools, characters in theatrical productions, and stories in Catholic Truth Society pamphlets.[43]

Contradictory liminalities of gender and physiology, not only thrive within these tales of Christian saints but also inform ways in which Catholics thought, and continue to think, about the power of the divine. Within the Catholic worldview, or what sociologist and priest Andrew Greeley describes as, the "Catholic imagination," the carnality of humanity offers the faithful a locus for engaging the divine. The Incarnation of Christ, His Passion, and Resurrection, among other central tenets of the Catholic faith (e.g., the Immaculate Conception and Transubstantiation of the Eucharist) rely upon the miraculous potential and malleability of the physical, human body.[44] Flesh becomes both the source for and symbol of religious piety. The *vitas* of female saints, most emphatically, provide a vivid structure for conceptualizing how flesh could reach sacred heights through experiences of both pleasure and pain. In fact, historian Caroline Walker Bynum posits that female saints and mystics exhibited the most corporeally theatrical constitutions with propensities for falling into trances and experiencing stigmata, levitation, and elongation or enlargement of parts of the body. She states, "Although both men and women manipulated their bodies from the outside, so to speak, by flagellation and other forms of self-inflicted suffering, cases of psychosomatic manipulation (or manipulation from within) are almost exclusively female."[45]

As importantly, acts of agency by women fulfilled a notion of "becoming male" as a means to accentuate Christian identity. In this mindset, maleness equated to redemption while femaleness aligned with fallen status and sin. Embodiments of sacredness or piety meant blurring gendered distinctions and thus, exhibiting "male" qualities. As a central trope in the stories of Christian heroines, "becoming male" allowed women to transcend gendered differences and access spiritual advancement.[46] While offering women an opportunity to "progress" toward holiness by adopting male agency and/ or physical attributes, this liminality also reinscribed gendered differences and their social divisions by emphasizing the most desired (male) position. Often, as in the case of St. Joan of Arc, the manipulation of gendered categories by women did not come without controversy or consequence.

These prescribed gender-bending connotations were not lost on Darger, as we shall see. He wove visual pairings of Christ with female saints into the backgrounds of narrative scenes as if setting contextual equivalences and references for unfolding Vivian Girl adventures. Through horrific illustrations of crucifixions and other extreme acts of altruism he conflates the girl body with that of suffering martyr, potentially even with Christ. Visualizing spiritual properties through the flesh of his little girl figure, a diminutive female, Darger raises the stakes to higher levels of sacredness and sentimentality as she becomes the ultimate site for suffering and Christian love. In the aforementioned opening passage of *In the Realms of the Unreal*, he offers an explanation for his choice of little girl heroines, arguing that,

> Little girls do and are brave enough, for a fact, to be able to play and show any amount of nerve and courage, full equal or moreso (sic) than boys or men or women who may take part in active warfare.[47]

He ends with this statement, reinforcing the absolute strength of the female sex: "Above all, in patient endurance of pain and suffering and sorrow, all women were and are immeasurably (sic) superior to men, and women always make sacrifices that men would think of in horror."[48] Note his emphasis on "endurance," "pain," "suffering," and "sacrifice"—terms more widely associated with martyrdom than childhood.

We find evidence of Darger's investment in these thoughts through his incorporation of the female saints dear to him, Joan of Arc and potentially, Vivia Perpetua, whose name and unique morphology closely resembles that of the Vivians. Both legends, SS. Vivia Perpetua and Joan of Arc serve as supreme exemplars within Miles' genre of "becoming male" and illustrate Bynum's assertion that fluid gendered associations overlay notions of female flesh and progressive advancement toward being one with Christ. However, the acts of Joan of Arc and Vivia Perpetua move beyond performances of bravery and self-abnegation into practices of cross-dressing (Arc) and renouncing motherhood and transgender epiphanies (Perpetua). Their significant stories destabilize the categories of gender and orient toward the goal of becoming male, thus, violating social boundaries while transcending their sex and earthly existence—a divine state which Miles finds explicit within the cult of the *virgo fortis*, or "strong virgin."[49] Darger embraces this gender-bending lineage familiar in stories of SS. Joan of Arc and Vivia Perpetua, exploiting their venerated, authoritative virility in order to fabricate his own holy and simultaneously, transgressive Vivian. Through sacred and available models, Darger envisions his little girl body as a powerful expression of piety and resistance.

Vivia/Vivian

Further consideration of "Vivian," connoting one who is a living force, intense, and brimming with vitality, turns this discussion to the declarative *vivam* (I shall live!); a cry of resistance, replete with associations of resurrection and super-hero transformation. Although Darger does not state the source of "Vivian," the possibility of this name's connection to "life" or "being alive" and the chances of Darger becoming familiar with *vivam*, *vivum*, *vivus*, or derivatives, *vivo*, and *vividus* through Catholic Mass seem likely.

Moreover, Darger's chosen family name for his seven protagonists follows a trajectory of vitality, endurance, and dispossession echoed within the name of female saint Vivia Perpetua. Theologians view the *passio* of St. Perpetua as a seminal document that shaped conventions for female sacred biographies since early Christianity.[50] Believed to be written in her own voice and that of another male, her *passio* worked to transcend the vulnerability and social stigma of her body, identifying with a heroic athleticism and spiritual integrity of "maleness." She was a woman who rose above her station and a mother who renounced motherhood, and like her name, resoundingly declared and demonstrated her Christian identity. Perpetua's acts serve as a template, showing that "Christian masculinity can be revealed in a most unexpected place: a woman."[51]

The life of Vivia Perpetua demanded nothing less than total surrender of mind and body to the Christian cause. Her progression from earthly concerns to otherworldly salvation begins with her conversion to Christianity and subsequent incarceration by the Romans in Carthage (203 AD). Ignoring her father's pleas to renounce her beliefs and to resume her motherly duty (to reunite herself and her nursing child with her pagan family), Perpetua prays for liberation from both. Divinity grants her petition by miraculously ceasing lactation and thus a physical (or "natural") link between her and her son. She additionally exhibits extreme resolve and volition by giving her son to her father. Unencumbered by family or male domination, Perpetua leaves behind markers of femininity. She becomes an active, religious agent, controlling her emotions and remaining firm to her faith, even as she faces her approaching death.

The masculinizing narrative of her story reaches its apex in Perpetua's fourth and final dream/vision and ensuing actions within the Roman arena. The night before her martyrdom, she dreams of entering the amphitheater to compete against an Egyptian, identified within her *passio* as the Devil. Stripped by assistants in preparation for battle, Perpetua is awestruck by her transformation into a male, muscular body. Her gaze drops to her genital region and she confirms her systemic manhood by uttering, "I became a man."[52] Perpetua literally saw herself as male.

Perpetua fully demonstrates Christ-like fortitude and sacrifice within the arena the following day after her transgender vision. Bravely encountering wild beasts and gladiators in the coliseum, she withstands the goring of a heifer. Unwilling to accept denial of her martyrdom's glory, Perpetua dramatically concludes her own life (retaining agency up until the point of her death) by guiding the sword of a hesitant gladiator to her own throat. Caught up in the rapture of her perseverance and corporeal duty, she shouts, "I am a Christian, and I follow the authority of my name, that I may be perpetual (*ut sim perpetua*)."[53] Martyrdom rejects the role of the victim. To die is to win. Even though Perpetua realizes she will stand before ferocious beasts in the coliseum, she envisions the confrontation as facing evil, and although dying, she will win. Vivia Perpetua delivers the imperious, somatic thrust of her victory in this linguistic moment.[54]

Religious Studies scholar, L. Stephanie Cobb extends and complicates Miles' discussion of fluctuating "maleness" in Perpetua's story by contesting assumptions regarding authorial voice and objective historical content in female martyrologies—Perpetua's, in particular. She argues that these narratives serve propagandistic, identity-forming functions within the early Christian community by demonstrating "manly," and thus "Christian" virtues, such as autonomy, athleticism, virtue, and stoicism. The Christian ideal appropriated Roman (pagan) attitudes toward gender and sex including, most importantly, a correlation between maleness and virtue, strength, and honor. Martyrs' Acts, even when narrating the works of a female saint, highlighted masculinizing tropes fueling these textual devices with persuasive, didactic stories illuminating what it meant to be Christian.

Cobb views Perpetua's transgender vision as another continuum of the literary trope within the narrative. Physical transformation identifying with maleness confirms what has already taken place on a deeper, sociological level. The phrase, "I became a man" offers an end cap to an earlier, potent remark made by Perpetua to her father, "I cannot be called anything other than Christian."[55] Her fourth and final dream, sanctified as a vision, allows Perpetua's image to play both sides of gender expectations, slipping back and forth between cultural notions governing male and female bodies. Her transformative body projects ambiguous, "female" messages vacillating between innocence, familial bonds, and physical weakness while creating associations with the male body—spiritual discipline, physical control, religious agency, and athletic victory.[56]

The power and punning quality of Vivia Perpetua's name, her transgender vision signifying perseverance and strength, and her legendary status as a conquering Christ-like figure, sets a divine, fantastic precedent for Darger's Vivian Girls. Perpetua's legend, like the story of the Vivians, challenges the normative way in which modern society views the relationship between sex and gender. Both operate on a sliding scale, moving between at one end, male, and at the other, female. Accordingly, both Perpetua and Darger's Vivian Girls demonstrate male attributes of athleticism and agency, while also exhibiting socially prescribed traits of female innocence and humble virtue.

Embedded within the extraordinary body of Perpetua and other virile female saints, one finds a "one-sex model" dominating anatomical thought prior to the eighteenth century. In *Making Sex*, Thomas Laqueur explains that epistemological discourse stemmed from one archetypal body—male: "Woman was understood as man inverted: the uterus was the female scrotum, the ovaries were testicles, the vulva was a foreskin, and the vagina was a penis."[57] Corporeal flux and gender resulted from production and retention of bodily heat, a "vital heat" regulating biological and social associations with male/hot (active) and female/cold (passive) properties. This "heated" logic encompassed a variety of biological functions, one specifically applied to menstruation and the transition from girlhood to womanhood. According to the one-sex model, women purged blood because their cold bodies produced a surplus of the nutriment (likewise, milk). Men, on the other hand, being "hotter," burned off such substances in greater quantities than women and, thus, did not menstruate.

Hierarchal binaries of male/female and active/passive, under the principle of vital heat, flourished throughout the medieval era and into the Renaissance, informing hagiographic portrayals of socially independent, female saints. "Hot" virile women (the *virago fortis*/strong virgin) of Catholic legend boldly transgressed gender boundaries, embodying power and prestige that was traditionally the reserve of men. Darger's running/morphing child draws from the heritage of the *virago fortis*, the defiant woman bearing male characteristics of active heat, vitality, and corporeal theatrics. This strong female elides within the playful metamorphosis of somatic boundaries between boys and girls in Darger's art. However, unlike phallic women within the frame of the one-sex model, Darger's girls rebuke the notion of being inversions of males, or less perfect boys. Vivian Girls never fully conform to the signs of male sex. They visually morph along a swinging pendulum, remaining for Darger, "little girls"—something entangling girl and boy, yet, privileging the girl. Perpetua's strange carnalities prepares a foundation for the Vivian, a point of departure already venerable, allowing Darger to further experiment with and discover the possibilities of gender-bending as a state of reaching oneness with Christ.

Warrior Maiden

> They fought . . . as if not only led by the spirit of the Maid of Orleans herself, but as if led by Christ and His Heavenly host of angels and Saints.[58]

By the time Darger alludes to the Vivians' driving spirit as akin to that of the "maid of Orleans" and inserts Joan of Arc's holy card into his imagery, Jeanne la Pucelle's legend has already reached the Catholic pinnacle of sainthood.[59] Her upwardly mobile image additionally reaches another elevation as secular spokesperson for the U.S. government's World War I effort.[60] According to cultural historian Ann Bleigh Powers, a Joan of Arc "vogue" flourished in America between 1894 and 1929. Periodicals and theatrical productions capitalized on America's growing interest in the girl saint. Many equated St. Joan's attempts (500 years prior) to drive the enemy from French soil with the patriotism of American soldiers in France during World War I.

Through the image of St. Joan, virginal innocence presented as a position of strength, a purity fighting contamination. Her representation entered an American discourse conflating childhood with religious virtue and patriotism decades before World War I. Mark Twain valorizes "little Joan" in his 1895 work of fiction, *Personal Recollections of Joan of Arc*. Joan's image also circulated around the globe as an androgynous youth in the popular children's book, *Joan of Arc* (1896, in French, 1918 translated into English) illustrated by Louis-Maurice Boutet de Monvel.

Darger's veneration of St. Joan as an emblem of female virtue embraces abstract elements of her legend, but more emphatically plays with particulars of her gender ambiguity and reputation as a *virago fortis*, or warrior maiden of the spiritual realm. Specific female aspects of St. Joan's martyrdom manifest in her virginity and defense of her chastity.[61] Her greatness, however, hinges upon extraordinary acts of bravery and a legendary body resistant to age and sexual differentiation. The legend of Joan of Arc asserts an incongruous virile femaleness ruled by an excessive spiritual conviction rivaling that of Christ. She transcends the limits of her gender while boldly asserting that fortitude and passion are not the exclusive properties of men.

Like the Vivians, who never age, Joan of Arc remained little throughout her short, intense life. Her saintly acts span a six-year period from age 13 (when she first heard voices) until her death at the stake at 19. Although her age and chosen name (*pucelle*) propel the maiden into womanhood, her legend safeguards her innocent, childlike persona. Hagiographies, especially those written in the nineteenth century, conflate St. Joan's life with the intertwining cults of the child and of the child Jesus, emphasizing her humble, bucolic origins as a shepherdess. Writers additionally cite reports of St. Joan's amenorrhea to confer her virginal state of prepubescence and holiness. French historian Jules Michelet concurs in 1844 that, "She had, body and soul, the divine gift of remaining childlike. She grew up, she became strong and beautiful, but she never knew the physical miseries of womankind."[62] Coupling this sustaining childhood with practices of transvestism (on and off the battlefield), with extraordinary bravery, and with a lifestyle devoid of conventional gendered obligations, St. Joan's image swirls within a conundrum. She is female, but she is not "woman" in social standing or physiological maturity. She dons male clothing and exudes spiritual passion, strength, and vigor—qualities associated with men. She embodies an innocent child, a holy (virginal) woman, and a fortitude approaching that of Christ. Cultural historian Marina Warner eloquently describes Joan of Arc's image as "sexlessness. . . . The state of suspension, of nondifferentiation, achieved by a transvestite girl . . . confirmed by the Christian tradition as holy."[63]

However, beneath this layer of holiness (and reinvention by the Catholic Church over centuries), lies the offending body of a girl who threatened to challenge the social prescriptions and boundaries of gender. Although most accounts of St. Joan's trial relate her verdict of heresy to the dubious origins of her miraculous voices and to wider international politics surrounding the Hundred Years War, Warner reminds us that St. Joan's inquisition steadily probed the manifestations of her "male" attire. The verdict, in part, demanded justice for St. Joan's social transgressions, finding her guilty of possessing the audacity to challenge the cultural constraints of her sex. The sexual ambiguity that elevated her status among Catholics, ironically, twisted into a confirmation of degenerate evil during the course of her indictment. Specifics of Joan of Arc's fiery death in 1432 suggest that the allure of (and fear of) her uncertain gender prevailed beyond her trial. An anonymous contemporary account records her death not as a spectacle of Christ-like suffering but as a violent interrogation of her ambiguous body:

> She was soon dead and her clothes all burned. Then the fire was raked back, and her naked body shown to all the people and all the secrets that could or should belong to a woman, to take away any doubts from people's minds. When they had stared long enough at her dead body bound

to the stake, the executioner got a big fire going again round her poor carcass, which was soon burned, both flesh and bone reduced to ashes.[64]

Rouen authorities chose not to strip Joan of Arc before burning her body. Along with purging her profane form, we might ask whether her executioners tested her mutable one-sex corporeality with intense heat, tempting a magical transformation? Bystanders expecting to see physical indications of her "maleness," instead witnessed a "poor carcass"—the blatant display of her "womanly secrets" degrading her divinity to counterfeit status. Darger's retold version of young female martyrdom does not disappoint with a revealed, ersatz supernatural being. The Vivian Girl transforms and elevates, visually confirming her thoroughly militant and "masculine" nature. She suffers like other Catholic female martyrs but does not find victory through death. In moments when fire or other destructive forces threaten her life or religious faith, she perseveres.

Executioners attested to finding Joan of Arc's heart, intact and engorged with blood, within the ashes. Symbolic of her integrity and devotion to God, this unconsumed heart, already pure, thus, impervious to purgation at the stake, retained the primary nutriment associated with vital heat. Her disembodied heart brimming with hot virility continues the phallic narrative of the *virago fortis*. Refusing finality, this remnant of body and soul performs a resurrection, decidedly more spiritual than corporeal, a familiar sacrificial logic akin to that of the risen and triumphant Christ.

St. Joan's influence is more emphatic as a contextual reference to Vivian Girl bravery and sacrifice in *At·Zoe-Du-Rai-Bech. The result after Violet saves a priest and his sacred monstrance from being shot* (Figure 2.4). In the left corner, adjacent to a drawn sculpture of a crucified Christ, Darger includes a framed portrait of a kneeling and praying St. Joan. The simple composition and St. Joan's clear, circular halo suggests that Darger traced this image from a prayer card. Her magnificent horse lingers behind her, turning to witness St. Joan's raised arms and penitent face. She pauses to pray before entering battle, evoking and re-enacting Christ's Agony in the Garden of Gethsemane. Within this interior scene, Darger places Joan in prayer next to an identifiable image of a crucified Christ, thus, staging a martyr-coupling. In the far right corner, a blonde Vivian Girl also falls to her knees and prays. Her gaze extends to the sacrificial pair of Christ and St. Joan. Next to this praying girl lies Violet Vivian, recuperating from a gunshot wound. Violet has taken a bullet to save both the integrity of a monstrance containing the holy Eucharistic host and the life of a priest. In this visual alignment, Darger pulls a symbolic thread, reading from left to right: Christ on the cross, St. Joan, and bleeding Violet. Violet, the leader of the Vivian Girls, in her altruistic act and suffering, resembles the pendant

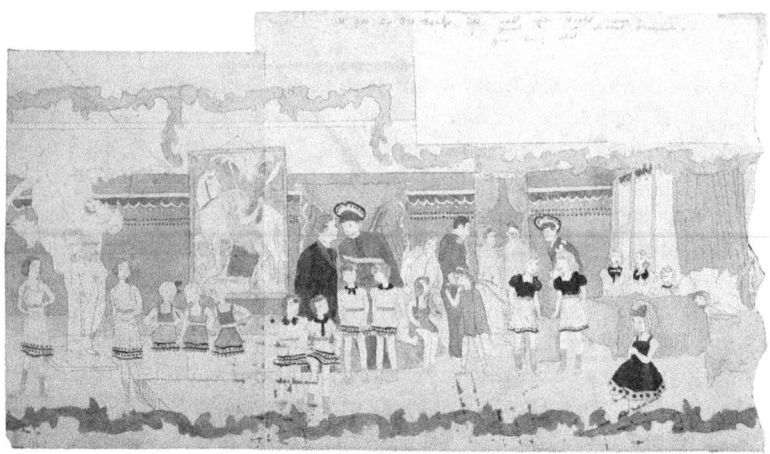

Figure 2.4 Henry Darger (1892–1973) © ARS, NY. At Zoe-Du-Rai-Beck. The result after Violet saves a priest and his sacred monstrance from being shot, n.d. Watercolor, pencil, and carbon tracing on pieced paper 48.26 × 86.36 cm. Private Collection, Belgium

Source: Courtesy of Andrew Edlin Gallery © 2020 Kiyoko Lerner/Artists Rights Society (ARS), New York

examples of Jesus and St. Joan. Additionally, the caption's reference to the intact monstrance, alludes to the Eucharistic sacrament of partaking the body of Christ and the miraculous liminality of the flesh.

This narrative panel employing St. Joan renders a familial kinship between the Vivians and a legendary female "girl" saint that exponentially expands with iconic and cross-gendering declarations. St. Joan calls the Vivians to perform virile transgressions of their female sex. She is Christ-like through actions and outer presence; her "virile" image merges with Christ, achieving oneness with divinity by expressing agency. In this sense, St. Joan's example does more than contextualize Darger's little girls; St. Joan legitimizes their role as sacred gender-benders. The Vivians (and other girls), like St. Joan, become active, phallic females blurring gender and commanding reverence. They wield a divine privileged body, marked as a recipient of grace, free from sin, and free from social constraints.

Adaptations of saints' names, martyr-narratives, and visual references to saints and Christ frequent Henry Darger's written tale and visual work. As I have noted in Chapter 1, Darger also employed the likeness of another popular "girl" saint, Thérèse of Lisieux as a model for Vivian behavior.

Furthermore, two of the seven Vivian Girls have floral names: Violet Vivian and Daisy Vivian—the very humble flowers that St. Thérèse celebrates in her journal as those "destined to give joy to God's glances."[65] Other saintly correlations have been noted by Michael Moon, in particular, the name of one character from *In the Realms of the Unreal*, Jennie "Anges," bearing a strong resemblance to the virgin martyr, St. "Agnes." He suggests though, that Jennie's horrific death—dismemberment by Glandelinians while saving a ciborium from defilement—is Darger's retelling of the story of St. Tarsicius, a boy beaten to death by a pagan mob for not giving up a ciborium containing the sacred host.[66] Agreeing with Moon, I also find St. "Joan" in "Jennie" Turmer, the girl who bobs her hair and dons male attire to slip through enemy lines. Moon surmises:

> The similarity of these names to each other and the way all of them proliferate across a significant portion of the major characters of *In the Realms* betoken a close identification on "Henry's" part—at least at the level of the name—with the various Annies and Jennies who undergo martyrdom in his text, as well as the virgin martyrs Agnes and Joan, whose names Darger's heroines cite and revise.[67]

To the growing list of Darger's retold Catholic tales, appropriated images and adopted names, I add "Vivian" and the heroics of virile female martyrs that defy gendered boundaries and "become male." Striking up visual parallels between Joan of Arc and Christ as well as somatic and linguistic associations with Vivia Perpetua, Darger marks his legendary Vivian Girls with intersexual signs announcing their sacred strength and religiosity. Prescriptive masculinizing tropes familiar to martyr narratives transform this epicene child into a diminutive warrior maiden, or *virago fortis*. As Darger reminds us, girls are braver than boys,[68] and Christian masculinity may be revealed in a most unexpected place—a little girl.

Notes

1 Portions of this chapter were previously published in "Vivam! The Divine Intersexuality of Henry Darger's Vivian Girl," *Elsewhere: The International Journal of Self-Taught and Outsider Art* 2 (May 2014): 24–42. The current chapter contains modifications and updates.

2 Written notation on a manila envelope, Box 72, Folder 11, Henry Darger Papers, American Folk Art Museum, Archives New York, NY.

3 MacGregor, *In the Realms of the Unreal*, 165–180.

4 While Darger did clip and save images of naked prepubescent children from sources such as women's journals and mainstream newspapers, his use of them as resources for his visual art was not consistent. Some of these images show marks from tracing around the edges of bodily forms. Others do not reveal

evidence of tracing. Resource material from the Henry Darger Papers, American Folk Art Museum Archives, New York, NY.

5 My use of the term "intersex" denotes a spectrum of sexual anatomy. According to the Intersex Society of North America, "intersex" can encompass a wide range of biological variation, including external sex characteristics that may vary in size, shape, and morphology. Differences in chromosomal combinations may also be included in this condition "in which a person is born with a reproductive or sexual anatomy that doesn't seem to fit the typical definitions of female or male." See "What Is Intersex?" Intersex Society of North America, accessed August 27, 2019, www.isna.org/faq/what_is_intersex

6 Quoted by MacGregor, *In the Realms of the Unreal*, 106 from Darger, *In the Realms of the Unreal*, Volume VII, 500.

7 Quoted by MacGregor, *In the Realms of the Unreal*, 95 from Darger, *In the Realms of the Unreal*, Volume X, Part I, 604.

8 Male genitals on little female bodies, although a strange sight, seem proportionate to their form. Darger does not exaggerate them or blatantly focus on the girls' pubic region.

9 MacGregor, *In the Realms of the Unreal*, 532.

10 Ibid. MacGregor writes, "in such ways as not knowing, the truth has a way of breaking through in disguised form. In Darger's case knowing and not knowing seem at times to alternate with the rapidity of a child playing peek-a-boo, now you see it now you don't . . . one is reminded of another childhood game played by little boys, that of hiding their genitals by tucking them back between their tightly compressed legs. . . . Obviously, other possibilities are too frightening to contemplate. With Darger, the regular appearance and disappearance of the penis in his drawings may reflect an unconscious playing with the levels of reality, a daring approach and retreat from the truth, which he does and does not know."

11 Referencing Anna Freud's theories, MacGregor argues that Darger's girl with intersex characteristics re-enacts the fantasy of a maternal phallus. He states, "Such a situation would seem to require reinforcement by trauma far in excess of that caused by the simple discovery of the crucial difference which distinguishes the sexes from one another. That trauma, in Darger's case, could have been supplied by the sudden death of his mother just prior to his fourth birthday. Whatever point he had attained in his psychosexual development, there is sufficient evidence to support a prolonged regression to, and fixation at, the anal-sadistic phase. This shock seems to have contributed to, and maintained, an unconscious awareness of an all-powerful and threatening phallic mother, now numinous because she was dead." Ibid, 533. Taking Darger's art as a literal embodiment of his psyche, MacGregor's "sufficient evidence" is his assumption that "at some level of his reality Darger believed that female children are equipped with male genitals." Ibid, 529.

12 Bonesteel, *Henry Darger*, 22.

13 Klaus Biesenbach, ed., *Henry Darger* (New York: Prestel Publishing, 2009), 13.

14 Moon, *Darger's Resources*, 20.

15 Ibid, 29.

16 Ibid, 79–80.

17 Quoted from captions in work by Henry Darger, AT SUNBEAM CREEK. Are with little girl refugees again in peril from forest fires. but escape this also, but half naked and in burned rags / At Torrington. Are persued by a storm of

fire but save themselves by jumping into a stream and swim across as seen in the next picture / At Torrington. They reach the river just in the nick of time. Their red color is caused by the glare of flames. . . (double-sided), mid-twentieth century, Watercolor, pencil, carbon tracing, and collage on pieced paper, 19 x 70 ½", © 2020 Kiyoko Lerner / Artists Rights Society (ARS), New York.

18 Ibid.
19 Ibid.
20 See Anderson, Plate 1 A, 24–25 for image.
21 See Anderson, Plate 6A, 42–43 for image.
22 The term "nuded" appears in captions, for example "At Jennie Richee. Assuming nuded appearance by compulsion race ahead of coming storm to warn their father." This particular caption associates "nuded" with running and morphing girls. Ibid, 43.
23 Thank you to my colleague, Dr. Eva Bares for this observation.
24 Quoted in MacGregor, *In the Realms of the Unreal*, 526.
25 Ibid.
26 The notion of "gender" is historically understood in opposition to that of "sex." While sex is assigned at birth (male/female), gender (masculine/feminine) is a matter of culture. Today, gender is viewed as a more complex and nuanced relationship to one's biology, self-identity as male, female, both or neither, and one's outward expression of gender. Accordingly, the definition of biological sex has also expanded to include a wider array of bodily characteristics. Gender and sex are no longer understood as aligned identities following a binary concept of only two prescribed determinations.
27 See MacGregor, *In the Realms of the Unreal*, 123, illustration 3.10.
28 Ibid, 169, illustration 3.55.
29 The majority of dated newspaper clippings within the Henry Darger Papers range from the 1950s and 1960s.
30 Henry Darger Papers, (Box 71, Folder 5).
31 MacGregor, *In the Realms of the Unreal*, 123.
32 The Coppertone Girl has been the mascot for Coppertone sunscreen in the United States since it was introduced in 1953. Created by Joyce B. Brand, a commercial pinup artist, this girl is known for her "innocent" expression of surprise as she turns around to look at a black dog that has pulled her pants down. The dog's actions reveal the little girl's buttocks and tan lines. Over the years, the Merck Corporation has altered the original image to show less of the girl's anatomy. Darger clipped versions of the Coppertone Girl advertisement from the *Chicago Sun Times* from 1963 and 1964. Other versions are undated and vary in scale. Henry Darger Papers, (Box 96, Folders 1, 2).
33 This work is part of the Collection de l'art brut, Lausanne, Switzerland. Illustrated in Biesenbach, *Henry Darger*, 160–161.
34 James R. Kincaid, *Child-Loving: The Erotic Child and Victorian Culture* (London: Routledge, 1994), 79.
35 Kincaid refers to the Coppertone advertisement as a paradigm of child-fashion and allegory of culture practice. See James R. Kincaid, *Erotic Innocence: The Culture of Child Molesting* (Durham: Duke University Press, 1998), 74.
36 Kincaid's overarching argument in *Child-Loving* asserts that notions of "the child" have been assembled in accordance with culture's desire over the past two centuries. Pedophilia (not always sexual but, sexualized) operates at the center of our culture, not at the periphery. "By insisting so loudly on the innocence,

purity, and asexuality of the child, we have created a subversive echo: experience, corruption, eroticism." Kincaid, *Child-Loving*, 4–5.

37 Examples of the girl-with-pail figure can be found in Anderson, 40–41; Plate 5B, "73 At Jennie Richee Escape by their help"; 50–51 Plate 8A "172 At Jennie Richee. Storm Continues. Lightning strikes shelter but no one is injured"; and 52–53 8B "Untitled (Vivian Girls Watching Approaching Storm in Rural Landscape)."

38 In a passage from *The History of My Life* from Monday, April 1, 1968, Darger wrote, "No April Jokes. Five Masses Including the Miraculous Medal Novena. Over Tanglement of Twine, Difficult to Do. Some Severe Tantrums and Swear Words. Sorry Saint I Truly Am. I Should Be Ashamed of Myself, But Am Not." Quoted in Bonesteel, *Henry Darger*, 250.

39 Some examples of holy card and sacred heart imagery in Darger's art include: a holy card of St. Thérèse of Lisieux and Sacred Heart of Jesus discussed in Chapter Two; *Untitled (Sacred Heart of Jesus)*, MacGregor, *In the Realms of the Unreal*, 327 and a Sacred Heart and Sacred Heart of Jesus, respectively in the *Main National Flag of Abbieannia* and the *National Flag of Angelinia*, Bonesteel, *Henry Darger*, 45.

40 See Miles, *Carnal Knowing*, 81–84.

41 Ibid, 55.

42 Ibid, 53–77.

43 Marina Warner notes that these stories were mostly passed down from nuns to girls in Catholic schools and female martyrs' names, even those from early Christianity, like "Perpetua," were honored as the chosen namesakes of nuns. See Marina Warner, "Memories of the Martyrs: Reflections from a Catholic Girlhood," in *Perpetua's Passions: Multidisciplinary Approaches to the Passio Perpetuae et Felicitatis*, edited by Jan N. Bremmer and Marco Formisano (New York: Oxford University Press, 2012), 348–365. Likewise, Michael Moon speaks to this practice of repeating Roman martyr narratives via theatrical productions in parochial schools that focused on the torture and suffering of female saints, as well as their, "exposed and curiously gendered bodies . . ." See Moon, *Darger's Resources*, 25–41, quote from 29.

44 See Andrew Greeley, *The Catholic Imagination* (Berkeley: University of California Press, 2000), 1–21.

45 Caroline Walker Bynum, *Fragmentation and Redemption: Essays on Gender and the Human Body in Medieval Religion* (New York: Zone Books, 1991), 186.

46 Several scholars argue that "becoming male" was a common trope in female martyr narratives. Many point to its ideological context within the Platonic notion of "oneness," a unified status, privileged over multiplicity/difference, equated with decadence and confusion. Others note the apocryphal, Gospel of Thomas in which salvation is made possible when the problem of sexual difference has been resolved. In particular, this passage is noted where Jesus is explaining this phenomenon: "When you make the two into one, and when you make the inner like the outer and the outer like the inner, and the upper like the lower, and when you make male and female into a single one, so that the male will not be male and female will not be female . . . then you will enter the kingdom." Likewise, this final passage: "Simon Peter said to them, 'Let Mary leave us, because women are not worthy of life.' Jesus said, 'Behold, I myself will lead her so as to make her male, that she too may become a living spirit like

you males. For every woman who makes herself male will enter the kingdom of Heaven." See Elizabeth Castelli, " 'I Will Make Mary Male': Pieties of the Body and Gender Transformation of Christian Women in Late Antiquity," in *Body Guards: The Cultural Politics of Gender Ambiguity*, edited by Julia Epstein and Kristina Straub (New York: Routledge, 1991), 29–49 and Craig Williams, "Perpetua's Gender: A Latinist Reads the *Passio Perpetuae et Felicitas*," in *Perpetua's Passions: Multidisciplinary Approaches to the Passio Perpetuae et Felicitatis*, edited by Jan N. Bremmer and Marco Formisano (New York: Oxford University Press, 2012), 54–77.

47 Darger, *In the Realms of the Unreal*, Volume VI, 262–263.

48 Ibid.

49 Although virginity is a staple in the category of female martyrdom, mothers could also enter this highest echelon of piety if they left behind the markers of motherhood and family, including children. Perpetua is honored despite of rather than because of her child. The masculinization of her character solves the question of her problematic relationship between maternity and sainthood. See Julia Weitbrecht, "Maternity and Sainthood in the Medieval Perpetua Legend," in *Perpetua's Passions: Multidisciplinary Approaches to the Passio Perpetuae et Felicitatis*, edited by Jan N. Bremmer and Marco Formisano (New York: Oxford University Press, 2012), 150–166.

50 Both Tertullian and Augustine referred to Perpetua's acts as a model of Christian courage and faith comparable to Christ's Passion. See Gail P. C. Streete, "Tough Mothers and Female Contenders," in *Redeemed Bodies: Women Martyrs in Early Christianity* (Louisville, KY: Westminster John Knox Press, 2009), 49–72.

51 Cobb, *Dying to Be Men*, 105.

52 Her vision alludes to the common practice of men stripping in preparation for athletic contests against beasts and gladiators. Persecutors stripped women to humiliate them before crowds and to capitalize on the spectacle of their bodies. Nakedness in religious doctrine also metaphorically disassociated men from society. Stripping off one's clothing equated to stripping oneself of possessions and familial ties. Legends of female saints titillate readers by stripping the female martyr multiple times and conversely finding miraculous ways to cover them.

53 Quoted in Miles, *Carnal Knowing*, 60.

54 See Judith Perkins, *The Suffering Self: Pain and Narrative Representation in the Early Christian Era* (New York: Routledge, 1995), 32.

55 Cobb, *Dying to Be Men*, 97.

56 Ibid, 102.

57 Thomas Laqueur, *Making Sex: Body and Gender for the Greeks to Freud* (Cambridge, MA: Harvard University Press), 236.

58 Darger conflates the leadership Joan of Arc with the Vivian Girls in this passage from *In the Realms of the Unreal*. Quoted in Bonesteel, *Henry Darger*, 21.

59 The Catholic Church canonized Joan of Arc in 1920. Darger began to write *In the Realms of the Unreal* around 1911–13. He began creating images in 1932.

60 Ann Bleigh Powers, "The Joan of Arc Vogue in America, 1894–1929," *American Society for the Legion of Honor* 49:3 (1978): 177–192.

61 Virginity as an ascetic practice and narrative trope diffused male fears about women's flesh. *Acta*, mostly written by male hagiographers, equate virginity with cleanliness akin to the state of Baptism and that of prelapsarian Eve.

62 Quoted in Warner, *Joan of Arc*, 19.
63 Ibid, 157.
64 Quoted in Ibid, 14.
65 Quoted in Frohlich, *St. Thérèse of Lisieux*, 35.
66 Moon, *Henry Darger*, 26 and 31–34.
67 Ibid, 38.
68 See introductory remarks featured in Chapter One by Henry Darger in Volume VI of *In the Realms of the Unreal*, 262–263.

3 The Power of Cuteness

The aesthetics of cuteness prevail in all of Henry Darger's little girls. The artist appropriates this particular brand of imagery from early to mid-twentieth-century coloring books, comic strips, and clothing advertisements. Sickly sweet with their small features, cork-screw curls and bows, each girl arrives at his drawing board ready-made with a look eliciting maternal love and protective cherishing. From these adorable doll-like figures, however, Darger fabricates diminutive warriors that lead armies, shoot weapons, and die in battle. Darger's art also takes a perverse turn as he shows these little girls tortured, bleeding, and disemboweled. The emotionally manipulative work of cuteness becomes apparent in Darger's unimaginable vision of cruel violence upon affectedly pretty children. Opposites that exist in Darger's world (aggression and helplessness; beauty and horror) are imposed on the cute object whose malleability produces an excess of concern for its well-being. While addressing Darger's employment of such ambiguous, yet provocative imagery, this chapter looks beyond codes of cuteness to locate its performative and conspicuous, commodified display in his visual art. Specifically, I turn to Darger's resources which include comics and other forms of popular media that speak to comparable, dramatic themes inherent in these cute representations—ranging from vulnerable children, namely orphans, and their associations with innocence, to related media-driven concerns about child abduction and murder. Seemingly powerless, the image of the cute little girl exudes a powerful aesthetic that manipulates the artist and viewer, alike. Her naive façade nurtures cuteness historically defined as, "cunning, clever, sharp, acute, and attractive in a mannered way."[1] As a cute object, the Vivian Girl's disavowal of power becomes her utmost power.[2]

Child Schema

Shortly after his first Vivian collage, and other experiments with hand-colored reproductions, Darger turned to the act of tracing and moved toward a more vibrant representation of childhood in the 1930s. Some of his favorite sources include coloring and activity books from Stephens Publishing Company (Sandusky, OH).[3] Page after page illustrate boys and girls engaged in playful activities: girls bake cookies and attend to flower beds while boys ride bicycles and take aim with slingshots. Immediately recognizable as children, these figures are represented with an economy of line that delineates small, soft bodies with short limbs and enlarged foreheads (Figure 3.1). Like the girl with a hoe, most have minimized facial features alluding to androgynous looks that repeat similar head/eye proportions, pouty lips, and perky noses. Sometimes even images of boys display noticeably long eye lashes. Here, in this coloring book page, long, curly hair and a large bow denotes her gender. Arrows and written directives let us know that she is a blonde-headed child.

Little girls in these coloring books often don stripes, polka-dots, and checkerboards offering a series of patterns that Darger assimilated and

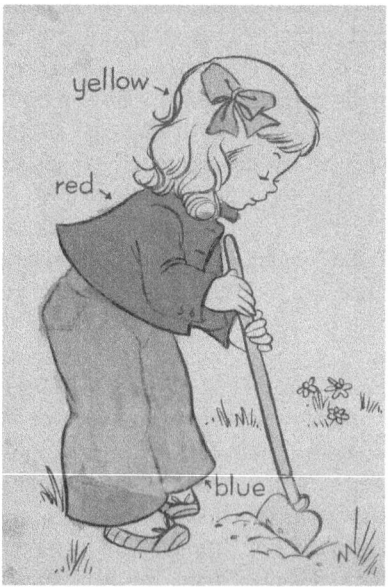

Figure 3.1 Henry Darger (1892–1973) © ARS, NY. Untitled (yellow, red, blue), n.d. Unknown coloring book page 11 3/8 × 7 ¾". Collection of Intuit: The Center for Intuitive and Outsider Art Henry Darger Room Collection and Archives

Source: Photography John Faier © 2020 Kiyoko Lerner/Artists Rights Society (ARS), New York

accentuated in his art. These decorative elements energize his landscapes populated by girls wearing frocks with mesmerizing, repetitive shapes. Tracing the girls' soft, curvilinear forms allowed the artist to transform still bodies into moving ones by extending legs, enlarging eyes, and opening mouths. What Darger appropriated from his resources was a remarkably vacant and pliable image ripe for reinvention and control. A few carefully traced lines along with minimal improvisation magically turned a Coppertone girl or a coloring book lass into a fantastic Blengin—a composite girl-figure with butterfly wings and curled ram's horns.[4]

The images Darger chooses to work with, whether illustrating a nursery rhyme or picturing playtime, are laden with meaning and connote the happiness, harmless fantasies, and unrestrained imagination that adults attribute to the blissful space of childhood. Indeed, one finds that these mainstream resources exude "cuteness" and "innocence" shamelessly. They are latent with nostalgic fantasies of an idyllic youth, empty and waiting to be colored in (adopted, if you will). For someone like Darger—a self-proclaimed "protector of children," attune to the call of these images—the coloring books offer a rich, fertile resource for illustrating his tale. The depicted children appear happy and healthy, and as evidenced by their clothing and situations, bear markers affiliated with white, middle-class America. The homogenous population of these coloring books provides multiple, vicarious ways for Darger to feed a desire to possess and perpetuate the look and feel of a childish utopia that he never personally experienced during his own childhood.

Coloring book imagery supplies more than just templates for the Vivians and thousands of other little girls in Darger's art. An array of cute things—children, puppies, kittens—pull at heart strings, but also signify socially constructed meanings and trigger psychological responses. Cultural historian Lori Merish views cute imagery as entangled within and productive of maternal desire, specifically motivated by "preservative love and protective cherishing."[5] Accordingly, cute imagery stimulates a response to identify with a little or miniaturized version of an adult in relation to its expected innocence and resulting vulnerability to corrupting forces. In an emotional call toward identification with the cute object, one feels a familial relationship, and, more importantly, an urge to care for its perceived helpless nature. Merish argues that cuteness mobilizes proprietary desire, a kind of psychological adoption producing the need to care for, cherish, and protect the object.[6] Cuteness is part and parcel of American consumerism, a catalyst attracting both children and adults to buy, own, and by extension, protect the commodified, cute object. A superlative example of this effect takes form within a doll, and for matters of this discussion, representations in coloring books and comics of little girls that look like dolls.

Scholars argue that an awareness of such internalized responses to cute markers originated in the 1940s with ethologist Konrad Lorenz's theory of *Kindchenschema*, or "child schema."[7] Lorenz posits that disproportionately large heads, big round eyes and soft bodies trigger innate releasing mechanisms of caring and related emotive responses in adults. Accordingly, other attributes of cuteness include a protruding forehead and elastic body surfaces, often resulting in clumsiness.[8] Cute imagery is more affectively involving and thus, attractive both visually and psychologically. In this example from Darger's traced sources, a study of a girl carrying a bucket (Figure 3.2), we see commonly cited attributes of cuteness: a large head and eyes, chubby cheeks and a braided hair-do that bounces along with her step. Likewise, she possesses a slightly plump body constructed of short, stubby limbs. Her feet, encased in Mary Jane-type shoes, appear to be too small for her top-heavy body. This girl along with at least two of the three disembodied heads to the right is probably appropriated from coloring books. Each portrays a variation of either a blasé or inquisitive-looking expression.

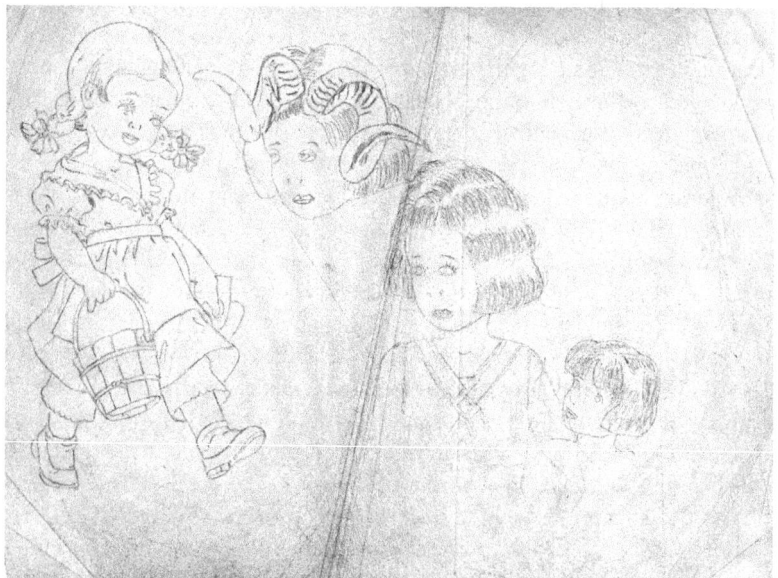

Figure 3.2 Henry Darger (1892–1973) © ARS, NY. Carbon tracing of girl with bucket and three heads Henry Darger Papers, Box 58, Folder 8. American Folk Art Museum, New York, NY, U.S.A.

Ram's horns adorn the first girl's head indicating that she may be a study for one of Darger's Blengins. The third head, at the far right, is that of comic strip character, Little Annie Rooney. The sheen from her coiffure and disproportionate features give away her likeness.

Cute imagery is ubiquitous in contemporary American pop culture and judging by Darger's archive of ephemeral material, the same was true for the early to mid-twentieth century. Certainly, the power of cute imagery lies in its abundance but also in its ordinary nature that easily transports from living child to inanimate, stuffed toy. This mobility allows cuteness to bridge real life and fantasy, making it an effective and relatable aesthetic in Darger's art. And, as Lorenz argues, the cute triggers affective behaviors that are learned and reinforced by mediated cultural codes,[9] many of which play out in commercial and media-driven imagery, the very base material comprising the Vivian Girls.

Spunky New Kids and Orphans—Rooney and Temple

Gleaned from the popular media of the 1930s through the 1950s, this brand of cute child provided Darger with a spunky, willful, and independent model, perfect for his adventures. Historian Gary Cross describes this emerging child type as the "New Kid"—a modern representation containing the markers of cuteness that kindled adult desires for adventure and the pleasures of consumerism. Accordingly, this child shed the previous century's romantic associations of his/her closeness to nature, inherent purity, and passiveness. Consequently, the allure of unquestionable goodness was replaced with positive emotional responses to the small child who was spontaneous, imitative, and precocious. Cross writes:

> By the beginning of the twentieth century, the idea of wonderous innocence had shifted from the romantic infatuation with nature to the delights of consumption, from a fixation on a timeless past to a fascination also with the future, and from a vision of the angelic child to a recognition of the naturally impish youth.[10]

In this new age of American consumerism, the cute became a selling point everywhere—children's fashion advertisements, on covers of the *Saturday Evening Post*, in comic strips, and on the movie screen. Cute, middle-class, white children were the portal for embracing the new. Commodified images of cute children were designed to appeal to adults who purchased toys and clothing for their own family. Cross notes a reflexive dynamic in this market-driven relationship between parents and their child where the child showed the way for adults to return to innocence, not through nostalgia but through purchasing all that allowed children to have the ideal childhood.[11] Adults desired (and still do) to protect their children by possessing and paying for commercial goods to make this ideal real.

In addition to coloring and activity books, Darger found this New Kid in the twisting and turning girls that model the newest fashions in clothing advertisements from Sears Roebuck and Woolworths department stores as well as in the diminutive features and defiant stance of "Little Annie Rooney." The *Little Annie Rooney* comic strip appeared in the *Chicago Tribune* from 1927 to 1966 and focused on the dramatic antics of a strong-spirited, fugitive orphan evading capture by a detective determined to send her back to a cruel orphanage. Rooney is cited as an obvious revision of Little Orphan Annie, launched in 1925. Michael Moon views Rooney as "a clear alternative" to Annie's narratives of self-reliance in that the strip "stresses . . . the extreme vulnerability of its child heroine."[12] Rooney sports a shiny, brunette bobbed haircut that accentuates her large head and nearly overwhelms her tiny nose and mouth. Facial attributes appear even smaller by comparison to her wide, black eyes. Despite her brunette hair, Rooney blends well into the army of blonde Vivians and their counterparts. Her leaner frame echoes that of the older Vivians and even more so, her narrative of orphan-adventurer, girl-on-the run shares a comparable theme to Darger's own story of independent, imperiled children.

In her research, art historian Mary Trent notes that Darger kept and archived several cells of the strip, *Little Annie Rooney*. Predominately from the mid-1940s to 1950s, these cells show the protagonist "reflecting on hardships and isolation."[13] For Trent, these images not only addressed concerns of the day, but also offered a relevance that Darger could internalize: "Though the strip ultimately presents optimistic messages, these cells indicate how it also grappled with serious traumas—poverty, orphanhood, child labor abuses, abandonment, loneliness—all of which Darger himself could relate."[14] Likewise, scholar Gavin Parkinson situates *Little Annie Rooney* into a wider arena when referring to what he terms, "orphan-adoption drama" narratives that Darger collected and absorbed.[15] He notes storylines in several comic strips beyond *Little Annie Rooney*, namely *Dick Tracey* (1931), *Mutt and Jeff* (1907–1983), and *Wee Winnie Winkle* (1920–1996), where children are abducted and/or reunited with an adoptive family. Given that the visage of Little Annie Rooney pops up everywhere in Darger's art, one can infer that she remained a pivotal figure for him, both aesthetically and conceptually. Her fugitive orphan-victim status and tomboyish nature align with multiple Vivian Girl qualities that allow them to succeed despite the trials and tribulations they experience in a hostile world. Parkinson muses,

> If Little Annie Rooney can be regarded as a mixture of cloying senti-
> ment and brutality, then it might even be said to have set a tone, beyond
> the specific details of its narratives, that was then amplified to taboo-
> breaking excesses by Darger in his paintings.[16]

Michael Moon also concurs with Trent and Parkinson. He emphatically spells out the ubiquitous nature of orphan-adoption narratives, noting the frequency of orphaned and endangered children threatened with kidnapping in comic strips and storylines of the early twentieth century. He explains:

> [W]hat has surprised me is the remarkable frequency with which
> orphanhood, kidnapping, and adoption recur as leading narrative
> motifs in the saga-style narratives of both elite and mass cultures in
> the early decades of the twentieth century—from the theatrical adapta-
> tions (and early films) of work by Charles Dickens and Harriet Beecher
> Stowe and their successor sentimental novelists to the Oz books, the
> newspaper headlines of Darger's youth, and many of the most popular
> early newspaper comic strips of the 1920s and 1930s . . . the abduction
> of orphans—the kidnapping of children who had no family to defend
> them from abduction or to attempt to track them after they had been
> abducted—was a problem that received widespread publicity in early
> twentieth-century media. . . . it is unsurprising that in such newly and
> massively popular comic strips as Gasoline Alley, Dick Tracey, Little
> Orphan Annie, and Little Annie Rooney, Darger and his contemporar-
> ies encountered an endless web of narratives in which often volatile
> relations among orphans, official caretakers, foster or adoptive parents,
> kidnappers, and policemen held center stage for weeks and months at
> a time.[17]

Following this consensus in thought, it seems likely that Darger found this New Kid type—cute, impish, and calculating—in the representation of orphans. However, one superlative example is largely missing in the scholarship on Darger and, again as I mentioned earlier, that example is Shirley Temple.[18] Without doubt, the popularity and commodification of Temple influenced the design, countenance, and behavior of Darger's Vivian Girl as it ushered in this new era of spunky cuteness. According to *Time Magazine*, Temple, at age 8 was "the world's most photographed person," appearing in newspapers and celebrity magazines daily and, even, competing for media-time with President Franklin D. Roosevelt.[19]

Her films consistently broke box office revenue records from 1935 to 1938, catapulting her star quality beyond that of any of her actress peers, child or adult.

Temple held a central place in the first decades of Hollywood film, particularly at 20th Century Fox where she starred in twenty-four movies from 1934 to 1940. After a series of films shorts from 1932 to 1934, dubbed "baby burlesques," Temple made her major debut with "Stand Up and Cheer!" (1934). According to historian John Kasson, Temple's performances promoted an optimistic vision of national recovery during the Great Depression. Her smile and fortitude promised deliverance from socio-economic strife not by changing the world but by summoning, "the emotional resources simply to persevere in it."[20] Temple's on-screen characters frequently play the role of an "almost" orphan who reforms adults with her naive, big-hearted optimism. Due to some tragedy or circumstance, Temple finds herself without a mother but secures one in a maternalized father figure. She emerges in her films as the lead actress, taking charge of the men around her, often wooing them as she sits on their laps. She plays the motherless girl (again, the very same type that Darger employs in his story), who softens and transforms a cantankerous widow or morally dubious bachelor.

Narratives of adoption and familial redemption begin with "Little Miss Marker" (1934) as Temple is left with a bookie after her father loses a bet on a horse race. Acting as a marker for his debt, Temple finds herself among a group of cynical men whom she eventually wins over. Temple continues to charm sardonic and downtrodden male characters throughout the rest of her films, most notably "The Little Colonel" (1935), "Captain January" (1936), "Heidi" (1937), and "Just Around the Corner" (1938).

Likewise, she's temporarily cared for or adopted by various gentlemen in "Now and Forever" (1934), "Bright Eyes" (1934), "Curly Top" (1935), "Poor Little Rich Girl" (1936), "Stowaway" (1936), "Little Miss Broadway" (1938), and "Susannah of the Mounties" (1939). Similar plots couple with wartime themes in the "Little Colonel" 1935), "Littlest Rebel" (1935), and "Wee Willie Winkie" (1937). These films featured recurrent themes of Temple as half-orphan, bouncing around from orphanage to home and among potential adult guardians vying to care for her. Kasson finds that similar plot lines throughout her films had a "long history in sentimental melodrama but an especially sharp pang in the Great Depression."[21] Temple, a disarming and cute child crusader, restores broken adult relationships, and as Kasson argues, she was a catalyst for "the repair of the sentimental economy of men."[22] Simultaneously, as a cute object, Temple frequently entices the audience to "adopt" her and vicariously occupy a motherly and cherishing role. Cuteness in Temple films is a spectacle with enough capacity to charm onlookers on film and in the audience.

America's love affair with Shirley Temple was not lost on Darger. Several items found in Darger's apartment confirm his share of society's infatuation with this child star. These items include a reproduction of a photograph (c. 1936) of Shirley Temple in a thoughtful pose—"your friend Shirley Temple" in printed script below[23] (Figure 3.3). Areas of faded color along with a light, handwritten address, "To Lorraine Witz" in pencil indicate that this may have been a stock image for a fan club member that Darger rescued from the trash. A large hole at the image's top center infers that he may have hung this stock photograph up on his wall. He also altered the image by blackening the reflective light in Temple's pupils with graphite. Perhaps, this was his way of replicating the large, black eyes and their familiar vacancy that he found in countless Little Annie Rooney renditions and coloring book girls. In addition to this image, kept intact for around thirty-seven years, he owned an illustrated book, *Shirley Temple: Story Book* (1935) filled with popular children's stories as well as two biographical texts. The first, *How I Raised Shirley Temple* (1935), is an account by

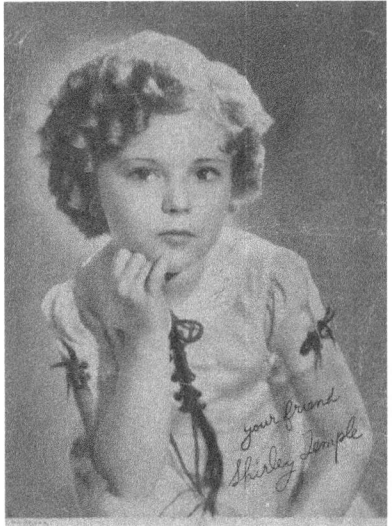

Figure 3.3 Henry Darger (1892–1973) © ARS, NY. Untitled (Shirley Temple). Digital print on photographic paper. Gift of Kiyoko Lerner. 2003.7.77

Source: Photo: Adam Reich. American Folk Art Museum, New York, NY, U.S.A. Photo credit: American Folk Art Museum/Art Resource, NY © 2020 Kiyoko Lerner/Artists Rights Society (ARS), New York

her mother, Gertrude Temple, featuring numerous photographs of the child star with her pets and other toys.[24] The other, *Shirley Temple* (1935) by biographer Jerome Beatty features a cover image of Temple in a formal, oval frame with a large bouquet of roses similar to Darger's own formula for his Vivian portraits.[25] These few publications owned by Darger are just a small part of a larger onslaught of commodified items featuring Temple's appearance and narratives designed to assert the normality and wholesomeness of this busy actress's life.

Darger fabricated his illustrated tale, while the films and marketing blitz of Shirley Temple profoundly shaped America's notion of childhood. At age 5 (1934), Temple made her feature film debut and shortly after, maintained a retail line of toddler attire that held its popularity well into the 1940s, even after she outgrew the toddler phase. Temple's accessibility provided an unprecedented visibility for children's clothing styles that designers and manufacturers capitalized on during the 1930s. Her toddler look is a defining attribute of Darger's girls: a small skirt or pinafore-styled dress that shows off a round belly and reveals the thigh, along with ribbons and other patterned accents to trim and reinforce what became known as a "toddler silhouette."[26] On the verso of *At Battle Near McHollister Run/At Wickey Sansinia* (Figure 3.4), the Vivians stand with their back to the viewer and peer into a panoramic distance. The gentle sway of their bodies, some with arms slightly extended and one in profile, mime stances from clothing advertisements providing clear views of the overall outline of their attire. Drab colors in their dresses blend into the background and highlight their legs, arms, blonde hair, and blue hats. The contrast of their white arms and legs draws

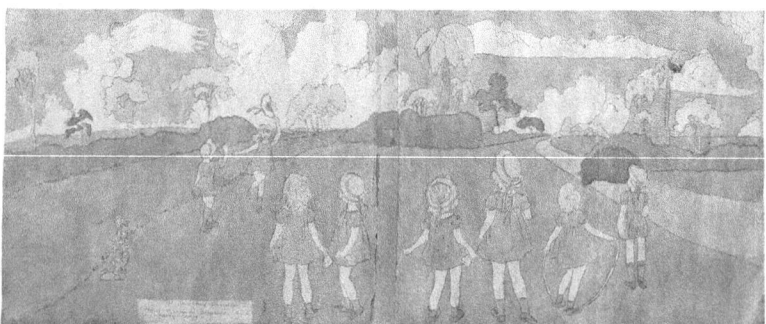

Figure 3.4 Henry Darger (1892–1973) © ARS, NY. At Battle Near McHollister Run/At Wickey Sansinia, mid-twentieth century. Watercolor and pencil on paper

attention to their short, toddler hem lines and sleeves. These kinds of Shirley Temple designs came in "Big and Little Sister" styles for ages 7–12 years— the very same age range of Darger's Vivians. In addition to the numerous advertisements in Sears Roebuck, Wieboldt's, and Woolworths department stores that Darger clipped and kept, he may have also encountered these "little" age ranges in articles from parenting magazines of the time.[27]

Along with the aforementioned memorabilia and Temple-inspired clothing designs and advertisements found within Darger's apartment, he also amassed multiple images of curly, blonde-haired girls that he displayed upon his fireplace mantel—a home altar organized around Madonna statuettes and other items from Catholic material culture (Figure 3.5). The angelic countenance of Temple and her look-a-likes seamlessly align with that of the Infant of Prague and other Vivian portraits hanging nearby. We find Temple's look and disposition everywhere in Darger's studio apartment and constructed world. She is visible within the artist's adaptations for the seven Vivians who sport Temple-inspired hair-dos, blue eyes, and

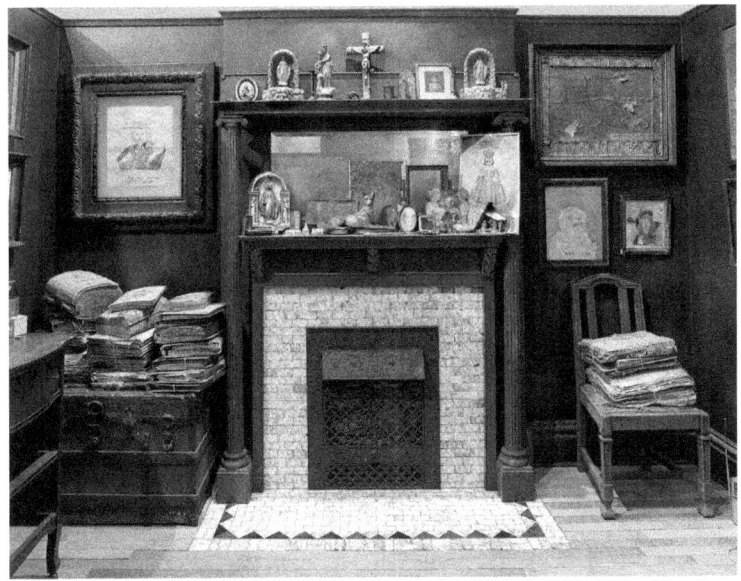

Figure 3.5 Henry Darger (1892–1973) © ARS, NY. Detail of Henry Darger Room installation at Intuit: The Center for Intuitive and Outsider Art. Collection of Intuit: The Center for Intuitive and Outsider Art Henry Darger Room Collection and Archives

Source: Photography John Faier © 2020 Kiyoko Lerner/Artists Rights Society (ARS), New York

thigh-high hemlines. As discussed in the first chapter, the artist's admiration for Temple is revealed when he references one of her most famous on-screen characters, the "Littlest Rebel" as an exemplar for girlish virtue in an introductory address to Volume VI of *In the Realms of the Unreal.*

Likewise, the self-awareness that the Vivians display, particularly Violet, signals Darger's desire to have these little girls play similar, Temple-inspired redemptive roles, however, on an extreme scale. In this passage, a tittering Violet considers her circumstances, conflating responsibility with acting. Darger writes:

> The terrifying drama of it all was over-whelming the little girl. Yet amid the chaos of clashing emotions, her ruling passion persisted. And she became agonizing aware that never before had she, nay any little girl or woman in any world's history of wars or other adventures been offered so stupendous a role to play before so vast an audience. . . . Her stage, the huge devastation theater of a World Record Breaking war; Glandelinians, and Holy God Loving Abbieannia, her audience, all the world looking on from the seats and balconies of the Grand Theatre, and all Kings and Queens.
>
> She giggled hysterically. Fascinated yet terrified, bewildered instinct urged her to seize the opportunity, and accept everything it offered— every peril, every pang, every great sacrifice, sorrow of parting with her sisters, maybe forever, even the bony embrace of death itself. . . . Comedy, melodrama, or tragedy, what did it matter, if she for the first time alone were to play the role, the supreme role of the World's History—the greatest of all heroines, the little heroine of heroines.[28]

Associations with cuteness emerge in Darger's descriptions emphasizing the "little heroine of heroines" and her unrestrained giggling. His written portrayal of the Vivians as cute characters is merely hinted at in passages like that mentioned earlier. More often than not the Vivians are described as beautiful in their appearance. Only in his visual art does cuteness reign as a dominant visual appeal for his Vivians.

Beyond representing the look and precociousness of childhood in the 1930s and 1940s, Temple's popularity centered on her ability to transform emotionally wounded men emasculated by their socio-economic status. Was Darger also so moved by his love and admiration for this little girl? Or, did he see in Temple's plots something of his own experiences? Kasson asserts:

> Shirley's repeated triumphs of healing, of building new families out of once broken hearts, spoke to audiences everywhere. Her feats carried special powers for those yearning for deliverance from their

families' miseries: poverty, prejudice, divorce, abandonment, alcoholism, derangement, sexual abuse—all of the woes of childhood. The darkest of these troubles, of course, never appeared in Shirley's films, but viewers in need could easily adapt her plots to fit their individual circumstances.[29]

The orphan's role in emotional healing is a trope extending beyond Shirley Temple's circle. Cultural historian Claudia Nelson contextualizes this poignant appeal of orphans within mass journalism's melodramatic stories that situated displaced children into "bleak and loveless environments" in which they were cast as the "embodiments of goodness—not as a target for reform, but as the motivating force behind it."[30] Orphan-based fiction, she asserts, presented a new "parent–child relationship, one that benefited the adult in an emotional rather than a practical way."[31] Concurrently, non-fiction reporting disputed the efficacy of orphanages maligned for their impersonal, soulless, and bureaucratic approaches to child-rearing. In the early twentieth century, the popular press along with numerous child aid societies and agencies promoted adoption and highlighted adoption's affecting and transformative potential for parents. Nelson explains,

> As toddlers have little immediate practical use, it was surely the little girls' emotional value that adoptive parents were acknowledging: their conformity to societal ideals of childish attractiveness and their presumed capacity, both as infants and girls, to give and excite love.[32]

Darger's need to be surrounded by the visage of little girls responds in many ways to society's message that welcoming children into the home was good and moral. These messages transferred into his story, a tale of Good vs. Evil, where the inherent qualities of little girls' virtue were certain.

Cute Deflections

A deeper look at Shirley Temple's appeal may also be instructive in thinking about Darger's own focus on little girls. Temple's coquetry, baby-doll outfits, and askance gaze were not understood as a veiled eroticism, much as we would interpret today. To the contrary, according to film studies scholar Kristen Hatch these aspects of Temple's performances were familiar and originated in late nineteenth-century American theater. In fact, children mimicking adult, sexualized behavior and the public proclamation of men's love for young girls, "functioned to assert the child's innocence, the impossibility of her experiencing or arousing sexual desire."[33]

The key to sexual deflection was inviting and acknowledging cuteness in the child performer. Temple preened, danced, and flirted while oblivious to sexual connotations. Consequently, men kissed, hugged, and placed her on their laps, sometimes repeatedly in films. The insinuation of a romance between Temple and her male costars was a convention in her films, understood as a wholesome, powerfully transformative relationship. Lori Merish, film historian, additionally confirms the deflective role of cuteness in Temple's performances:

> Staging cuteness as a mini-seduction met not by sexual violence or assault, but by protective care these films reinforce a primary mythology of patriarchal 'civilization' . . . that the overtly sexual scenarios and references in Shirley's films did not scandalize 1930s audiences suggests less the fabled 'innocence' of those times than the structure of sexual disavowal in which the cute Shirley was embedded.[34]

Hatch explains that during the course of Temple's rise to fame, such child worship was "understood to have a beneficial effect on society."[35] She writes,

> Men were applauded for befriending the young girls of the stage or even adopting them. For, rather than suggesting pedophilic desire, these accounts of 'child-loving bachelors' celebrated men's readiness to pursue innocent pleasures rather than the more bawdy ones on offer in the mass media.[36]

Indeed, Hatch admits that these kinds of reactions to the performance of girl stars, specifically Shirley Temple, would be "unimaginable to twenty-first-century audiences."[37] However, as Temple's innocence remained protected within Hollywood frameworks, competing conceptions of innocence coexisted in commercial culture and scandalous news stories. Hatch points toward another developing model framed by Freudian notions of adult sexual repression that began to take hold in popular discourse. Childhood innocence was thought to be transformative and powerful up until post-World War II years when attitudes changed and adult sexuality placed innocence in constant danger of being corrupted. By the end of Temple's career, innocence was no longer impervious to sexuality; it became absorptive, contested, and seen continually under threat.

The appeal of Temple's cuteness came from the fact that her disposition slid between the naive-dependent and the wise and coquettish flirt. By the same token, Merish argues that Temple's impish charm was further enhanced by racial markers and her contrast with African Americans on screen, specifically with Bill Robinson.[38] Often portrayed as a singing and dancing duo, Temple's and Robinson's relationship operates as a complementary foil of opposites. "Uncle" Billy represents the stereotyped, emasculated black male of a mythologized plantation past. Conversely, Temple, his social superior, embodies precocious perfection.

Merish presses the point further, noting that Temple's gleaming whiteness not only defines her cuteness but also assigns her value, elevating the desire of adults to protect her. She argues that adult attraction to Temple's white cuteness, "is reliant on the stirring of a protective impulse, a motive generated unfailingly in Temple's films as she is nearly always in need of adult care, despite her claims to the contrary."[39] Temple's on-screen quasi-dependency and ability to inspire adults equally manifests in the Vivians as they lead Christian armies and are at times rescued from certain death by soldiers. Likewise, Darger's Vivians not only look and act like Shirley Temple, they also radiate with a glow of whiteness, a larger metaphor for their infallible purity and goodness. Men everywhere in *In the Realms of the Unreal* venerate the Vivians and desire to keep them safe. Jack Evans, a Christian soldier and chaperone of the girls, frequently gushes over the Vivians with hyperbolic sentiments. This soldier describes these girls as, "etherically (sic) beautiful" wearing the most "beautiful white guasy (sic) dresses, whiter than the most great whiteness could ever be dreamed of." He further conflates their attire with a celestial aura as he additionally notes that the "strong moonlight surrounded them with a soft radiance."[40] Darger's words relay the translucent qualities of whiteness that suffuse and surround the girl bodies, expanding their valuation and culturally encoded aesthetic. His descriptions convey an understanding of white racial markers as visages of transcendent beauty.

Homogeneous renditions of girls and other characters in Darger's art present a sense that his imagery is devoid of race; however, my inquiry finds that beneath the blank, unblinking façade of his girl characters a particular history of white and black representation emerges. Darger's favored little white girl typology draws from a lineage of white bodies constructed and elevated by racialized polarities. We find this dynamic in Temple's "The Littlest Rebel" as well as in numerous other, "Old South" films where she is frequently partnered with an African American male, playing the role of a servant or in most cases, a slave. Many scholars of African American art and culture, specifically Jo-Ann Morgan, trace the racial dynamics within the roles played by Shirley Temple and Bill "Bojangles" Robinson to the pairing of Uncle Tom and Little Eva of Harriet Beecher Stowe's *Uncle Tom's Cabin, or, Life Among the Lowly* (1852).[41] As I have demonstrated, Darger greatly favors Little Eva, who he uses as a measuring stick for Christian love and morality in descriptions of his own Vivians.[42] He also acknowledges the

Vivians' father–daughter relationship equating them with Little Eva's paternal bond—a union reminiscent of the familial ties in Temple's films and similar patterns of girl–adult male dyads running through Darger's prose and his library of children's literature.

The pious perfection of Little Eva is played off of the minstrel-like, grotesque figure of Topsy in Stowe's novel. Topsy embodies the black caricature of an inept and wild, yet naively innocent slave. Stowe writes, "There stood the two children, representatives of the two extremes of society. The fair, high-bred child, with her golden head, her deep eyes, her spiritual, highbrow, and her prince-like movements; and her black, keen, subtle, cringing, yet acute neighbor."[43] This contrived opposition of racialized girl bodies from Stowe's novel evolved into a popular doll at the turn of the century. Originally known as "Topsy-Little Eva" dolls, this toy was composed of two partial bodies: one, white, in an antebellum style dress and the other, black, bearing an apron. This doll's overt and self-defining white/ black racial doubling was later re-directed by a slight name change—an implied reference to its flipping inversion as "Topsy-Turvey" dolls.[44] Due to their rigid construction, the halves of this doll could never play or converse with each other. Each half fully concealed the other that waited, latent under and inside it. Like the performances of Shirley Temple, this doll operated on a relationship of binary contrast.

Looking at Darger's depictions of little girls, we find a blank, white, or "uncolored" (in a coloring book sense) skin tone. This space which offers itself as a seemingly neutral backdrop to blonde ringlets or black bobs and blue eyes does, in fact, profoundly shape his protagonists. Each girl is heir to the notion of whiteness as a universal stance that normalizes and naturalizes her appeal and power. As scholar Richard Dyer reminds us, whiteness is frequently perceived as an invisible racial position. He argues that "race is something applied to non-white peoples" and thus white individuals stand for and embody the "commonality of humanity."[45] This kind of agency—to speak for the human race—carries with it a power to control representations of not only whites but also non-whites.

We don't know Darger's position on politics or racial differences. However, the polarized racial doubling that constructs little girl whiteness within pop culture paradigms lies latent within Darger's Vivian Girl. These little white girls, fashioned from and measured against existing popular representations of American childhood, participate in a wider cultural production and consumption of a particular, racialized and idealized type of girl. Although entangled within this racialized history of representation, Darger's cute child possesses a special ability to seemingly conceal race, as well as repel sexuality. Their blonde-haired, blue-eyed image skillfully operates within modes of deflection rather than absence.

Coexisting Paradigms of Innocence

Kristen Hatch's argument concerning early twentieth-century constructs of innocence runs contrary to that of scholar James Kincaid, who attests that Victorian culture fabricated an inherently erotic vision of childhood while also creating the pedophile as a scapegoat and diversion from Western society's investment in "child loving."[46] As I previously address, the coy Coppertone Girl partially revealing her buttocks is one of Kincaid's prime examples of American culture's uneasy fascination with children. Shirley Temple also makes his list. For Kincaid, Temple's adorable ways play out society's erotic fantasies about little girls:

> [S]he is blessed by nature not with beauty but with a total emptiness, a fat, round face with nothing in it and a body to match . . . into that vacancy audiences could project what they wanted, and what they wanted included voyeuristic pleasure . . . And Shirley Temple's comic strip-like being demanded so little for itself that it was easy to read into it the negations we wanted, innocence and purity.[47]

While Kincaid's opinion may counter Hatch's notion of the redemptive power of little girls in cinema, his words concerning the abuse of children offer a pathway for grasping concerns projected in the mass media that affected Darger while creating *In the Realms of the Unreal* and his follow-up untitled novel. Kincaid bluntly states,

> Our culture has enthusiastically sexualized the child while denying just as enthusiastically that it was doing any such thing. We have become so engaged with tales of childhood eroticism (molestation, incest, abduction, pornography) that we have come to take for granted the irrepressible allure of children . . . we do not pretend that we are getting the problem under control; quite the contrary. We know we are dramatizing the issue, making it into spectacle.[48]

Darger encountered dramatic narratives of child kidnappings and murder in two significant ways: (1) through the *Chicago Daily News* and other media outlets reporting real-life abduction and death of little girls and (2) through a religious context in a publication from the Archdiocese of Chicago, *My Child Lives*. News coverage, particularly that of 5-year-old Elsie Paroubek's murder and its influence on Darger's art have been at the forefront of much scholarship while the publication, a book from Darger's library, has not.

Darger conflated his real-life experience of misplacing Paroubek's 1911 newspaper clipping with the storyline of a lost martyred-child's photograph

In the Realms of the Unreal, dubbing it the "Great Aronburg Mystery."[49] Paroubek went missing on April 8, 1911, while on the way to a family member's home in Chicago. News reports stated that she was lured away by an Italian organ grinder and later taken away by gypsies spotted in a wagon on Kedzie Avenue.[50] Detectives and vigilante groups searched gypsy camps along the Des Plaines River for the next month. Her body was found in a canal on May 9. The papers noted that this "little girl" with "long, curly golden hair, blue eyes, and pink chubby cheeks with a prominent dimple in each" died from strangulation not drowning.[51] Her murder still remains a mystery to this very day. The *Chicago Daily News*, among others ran her image on the front page. Darger kept this newspaper photograph and later lost it. Scholars note Darger's written (and plausibly verbal) threats to God for its return with ultimatums declaring an alternative ending to *In the Realms of the Unreal*. This ending would allow the evil Glandelinians to triumph and eliminate any possibility of a Christian victory. Threats were accompanied by prayers, novenas, and even Darger's construction of an altar.

Michael Bonesteel initially linked Paroubek to an avatar, Annie Aronburg, the first murdered child-martyr in Darger's story.[52] Aronburg's murder initiates the child insurrection, while the "mystery" of the missing photograph (a fictional object lost by General Darger in *In the Realms of the Unreal*) and Aronburg's spirit haunts characters throughout the remainder of the story. Bonesteel reads the parallel narratives of the loss of a prized photograph by both Darger and the fictional General Darger as a manifestation of a loss of the artist's religious faith culminating in "violent fantasies of revenge" against girls and Christian armies as well as an unresolved conclusion for the story.[53]

John M. MacGregor, however, sees these parallels as evidence of Darger's psychosis and his inability to reconcile grief and difficult circumstances in his life. Specifically, he associates the loss of the photograph with the loss of Darger's sister,

> the little girl that he never saw, whose name he never knew . . . Elsie Paroubek functioned briefly as a symbolic substitute for his lost sister. That she was murdered, strangled, is also not without significance. . . . His obsession with the dead Annie Aronburg and her lost picture was also powered by real loss, though probably without Darger being aware of the connection. . . . The intensity of his longing for this lost little girl, renamed Annie Aronburg, resulted in a bizarre, indeed pathological process of identification with her.[54]

Mary Trent, however, argues that Darger's fascination with Elsie Paroubek is not only a solipsistic exercise. Interest in grisly crime stories and lost children in the news are not only inherent to the artist's own fetishization of the innocent child, but also "... address topics of concern and modes of representation that were prevalent in the visual culture of the time."[55] Noting several examples within Darger's ephemera of clipped photographs and news coverage of girl victims she states, "These girls . . . are perfect illustrations not only of a fetishized ideal of childhood purity but also of adults' overactive anxiety over its violation."[56] The translation of this anxiety in the imagined case of the Aronburg Mystery is yet another powerful affirmation of the allure of childhood innocence and its vulnerability. And, although not implicitly stated, Trent's words hint at scholars' own apprehension and uneasiness with stories of child abduction and murder, even if fictional.

Likewise, Moon reminds us that several stories of child abduction emerged in the popular press during Darger's youth and adult life. Most notably he cites, the "great Arizona orphan abduction" of 1904, in which a New York group of nuns from the order of the Sisters of Charity attempted to place forty orphans around the ages of 3–5 with Roman Catholic Mexican families in the Southwest. White protesters intervened and abducted/adopted the white children.[57] Moon makes the point that child abduction was not exclusive to affluent society, such as the infamous Lindbergh child abduction in 1920. It was a widespread issue heavily followed by the media, and as such, a significant and rich source for Darger's own storyline.

Equally provocative and shaped by sensationalized news stories, *My Child Lives*, subtitled, *Consoling Thoughts for Bereaved Parents* is a bound, hardcover book written by Reverend Alphonse Louis Memmesheimer of the St. Francis de Sales Parish, printed in 1937. Darger owned a first edition copy.[58] Chapter 4 offers several biblical examples for mothers to help them understand the tragedy of losing a child to either kidnapping, death, or both. It foregrounds the torture and murder of the Maccabean brothers, King Herod's killing of Holy Innocents, and the martyrdom of St. Felicitas's children. In each case, bereaved mothers are praised for their bravery and likened to pious behavior of the Virgin Mary. Midway through the chapter, the narrative shifts to current day concerns as the author simply states,

> Perhaps the keenest of life's sorrows is having one's child kidnapped and slain . . . The full extent of their sufferings is known to God alone. We can judge merely from the pitiable condition in which their little bodies have so often been found.[59]

Several scenarios follow including tales of children being lured away by strangers with candy, desperate parents pleading for the return of their child in radio addresses and published letters, and dozens of cases of crimes against children reported in the paper. Many of them include lurid descriptions accentuating the innocent nature of the victims and read like the short article on Paroubek. The multiple examples are direct and horrific. Here are a few:

> Two sisters, six and seven years old, were criminally attacked before they were locked alive in the ice box in their ranch home and left to suffocate . . .
>   Girl, Eight, Seeking Lost Pet, Lured to Cellar, Slain . . . In search of her white 'bunny' which had hopped away . . . beat her over the head with a whiskey bottle and attacked her.
>   Her body completely dismembered and sewed up in a bag, a girl of twelve was returned to her mother.[60]

The chapter ends by contextualizing the child's suffering within martyrdom and the mother's to that of Mary's, or the Maccabean mother: "Bear up, be courageous as these noble souls!"[61] Accordingly, the promise of resurrection remains for children slain and mutilated because of their innocent soul.

In Darger's story, the death of children and its religious significance is also addressed with a similar sensationalized rhetoric of both media-driven narratives and the prose of *My Child Lives*. However, his version of a spiritual path for the deceased departs from Catholic doctrine. Slain children, in a manner consistent with *My Child Lives*, equate to Holy Innocents but transform into "other Christs" as Darger notes:

> If this story were true, these, also probably among victims of massacre, disasters and dying child-slaves would be chosen bands in heaven, so like the Holy Innocents, First Flowers of Christ's coming, yet so different, who would be terrible witnesses against all things recorded already in these many volumes so far. . . . The beauteous bands who either in reality, or in this story, followers of the Lamb withersoever he goeth would have been made up of Dear Children, who might evidently after death, been changed into other Christs, by early communion, and brought our Blessed Lord's intercession in behalf of Abbieannia and her Holy states, and bring such a downfall of a wicked nation like Glandelinia, that Babylon, Rome, or other wicked countries never experienced, and in a way that would flabbergast the world and astonish all historians, and writers, and all college professors including, I the author.[62]

Focusing on martyrdom, spiritual ascension, transfiguration, and intercession, this paragraph as a whole encompasses how the work of the Holy Spirit is described. The context of "First Flowers" as signs of Christ's coming may be a conflation of Darger's association of little girls with flowers and a reference to the "first fruits," a renewal of purpose felt by the Apostles after being anointed by the fire of the Holy Spirit at Pentecost. Galatians

5:22–23 reads, "But the first fruit of the Spirit is love, joy, peace, longsuffering, gentleness, goodness faith, Meekness, temperance: against such there is no law."[63] The text, *My Child Lives*, likely provided a bridge between current-day anxieties about murdered children and Darger's religious piety. For the artist, white girlhood was a holy, privileged state, a pliable and liquid embodiment full of evocations of Holy Spirit, resurrection, and sacrifice. From death, children re-emerge transformed and victorious as *other Christs* through acts of intercession by the Lord. Darger additionally applies this super-fluid statement of faith to the world outside of his art, slain *Dear Children*, either *in reality or this story*.

Cute Bodies Invite Violence

Death, suffering, and horror fall outside of the moral boundaries of typical cute affiliations; however, they intersect with and infuse further meaning into cuteness in Darger's world. We can begin to unpack this intersection in gruesome passages from *In the Realms of the Unreal* describing the murder of a 7-year-old girl—the epitome of vulnerability:

> [T]hey tore her clothes till she was completely naked, they showered blows upon her, cursed her, strangled her, pulled out her tongue, hair, and eyelashes, and kicked her in the stomach, and struck her in the face and jaw with their fist, and pulled out her hair, and tortured her most horribly. . . . At last an infuriated ruffian fell her with a blow of the heavy musket butt, and the others completed the work with their bayonets, literally laying her body open.[64]

She, like thousands of little girls, perishes with such vicious intensity. The creation of a violent fantasy world that indulges in such shocking details raises many questions about the artist's motivations. However, these details, beyond their reciprocal exchange with current day girl-victimhood stories in the media and Catholic publications for bereaved parents, reveal another dimension of cuteness and its ability to harbor a potential for acts of cruelty. Cultural historian Daniel Harris argues:

> Because it aestheticizes unhappiness, helplessness, and deformity, it almost always involves an act of sadism on the part of its creator, who makes an unconscious attempt to maim, hobble, and embarrass the thing he seeks to idolize.[65]

Disproportionate features and bodies relay a kind of distortion, linking the cute to the grotesque and pity. One feels sorry for the cute thing, or "loveable inferiors" who elicit a "seductive and manipulative aesthetic that arouses our sympathies."[66] The vulnerable nature of cuteness produces ambivalent responses, an affective aesthetic that according to theorist Sianne Ngai exists in an object, "often intended to excite a consumer's sadistic desires for mastery and control . . . as much as his or her desire to cuddle."[67] Cruelty lies latent within cuteness. Harris states,

> Although the gaze we turn on the cute thing seems maternal and solicitous, it is in actuality transformative and will stop at nothing to appease its hunger for expressing pity and big-heartedness, even at the cost of mutilating the object of its affection.[68]

Within the cute object of Darger's world opposites coexist in a symbiotic relationship. One's experience of tenderness can quickly shift into aggression, even violence. Harris's and Ngai's arguments pertaining to the dark side of cuteness are helpful for understanding Darger's sadistic imagery, specifically that of little girls in distress, being tortured, or murdered.

In both word and image, Darger revels in acts of cruelty, often and most tellingly, against little girls sporting their polka-dotted dresses and bows or naked except for their Mary Janes. He frequently places girls in a wholly unpredictable and menacing environment. Implicit violence becomes part of the experiential pleasure of Darger's appropriated cute girls. In many ways, his art insinuates that cuteness operates as a façade for deeper, more sinister and cunning proclivities. Indeed, our immediate and piercing maternal response to cuteness makes us suspicious of its exploitative nature. The aesthetic of cuteness manipulates Darger as well as viewers, even though we are aware of and find pleasure in its artificial pull. In written passages and visual works featuring violent scenarios, Darger alerts us to cuteness's proximity to the grotesque—a kindred aesthetic in its malformed appearance, uncontrollable dimensions, and complicity with pity.

Without doubt, Darger's depictions of little girls tied up, naked, and sometimes with intersex characteristics seem so at odds with his appropriation of saccharine, cute resource material and child-worshipping language. Given the Teflon quality of Temple's innocence, again *the* model of girlhood and an obvious inspiration for Darger's construction of little girls, we can see how these incongruent aspects of girlhood thrived concurrently in Darger's art and his concerns for abducted children. Like the performances of Shirley Temple, cute aesthetics embedded within Darger's little girls radiate ambivalent and ambiguous qualities—warmth, innocence, and goodness, as well as those tied to their almost-orphaned status—vulnerability and fragility. Mixed sentiments of love/affection and pity/compassion exist within the core images and narratives that Darger appropriates. Lurking dangers and death at the hands of Glandelinians heighten these cute qualities latent within Darger's protagonists as they appeal for protection to Darger, his cast of characters, and his subsequent audience. And, as we look at Darger's art with twenty-first-century eyes, we must be aware of competing logics of innocence that coexist in his depictions of little girls. One, an innocence embedded within Shirley Temple and other actresses from early twentieth-century cinema that is redemptive, especially for men. This kind of innocence is beyond reproach and the other, an innocence that is inherently erotic and sensationalized—the "child loving" phenomena argued by James Kincaid.

In the previous chapter, I have interpreted violence and children with intersex markers in Darger's art through the lens of Catholic martyrdom's transformation and transcendence of the body. I cite, among other precedents, the miraculous transgender dream of Saint Vivia Perpetua and the ambiguous gender of Saint Joan of Arc. Overlaying the aesthetics of cuteness onto this interpretive lens tells us something deeper is at play in Darger's art. The "cute" body morphs from a sympathetic form (eliciting maternal desire) to one that produces empathy, bringing the reader/viewer into the mindset of Christian armies enraged by the sight of dismembered and disemboweled children. How better to motivate adults to equal levels of violence (those Christian armies within the story) or to engage readers throughout 15,000 pages of text than to threaten to destroy what they believe is of the utmost precious and sacred? Thus, cuteness divides its power accordingly in *In the Realms of the Unreal*. Vibrant cute bodies garner pleasurable, emotional responses that are warm and reaffirming. The brutally murdered or tortured cute body demands reciprocal, violent action, as well as provides a kind of sadistic pleasure inherent to its clever appeal. Both the life and death of "the cute" in Darger's world justifies its cultural value.

Darger's exploitation of cuteness to elicit different responses reveals the artificial nature and ambiguous qualities of this culturally encoded aesthetic. Appropriated from a commodified and thus already desirous adult gaze, cute characters in his art invite affectionate involvement and congenial feelings. They also become a site for both establishing and testing the polarities of goodness and cruelty, power and vulnerability as well as innocence and sexuality. These extremes underline and make clear the motivations for his seemingly endless war, which leads to the eventual triumph of a new girl order.

Notes

1 "Cute," Oxford English Dictionary, Accessed March 10, 2020, https://www-oed-com.proxy177.nclive.org/view/Entry/46355?rskey=GtWQvQ&result=3&isAdvanced=false#eid.

2 I have taken liberties with a quote by art historian, Elizabeth Howie to accentuate the importance of disavowal in Darger's employment of cuteness. "Cuteness thereby engenders its own discipline by enforcing particular behaviors of the

viewer; in turn, it engages and disciplines its viewer. Its disavowal of power is one of its powers." Elizabeth Howie, "Indulgence and Refusal: Cuteness, Asceticism, and the Aestheticization of Desire," in *The Retro-Futurism of Cuteness*, edited by Jen Boyle and Wan-Chuan Kao (New York: Punctum Books, 2017), 56.

3 The Henry Darger Room Collection and Archives at Intuit: The Center for Intuitive and Outsider art contains numerous examples of coloring books from the Stephens Publishing Company. Some are fully intact while others were used by Darger as scrapbooks for preserving news stories and images for his artwork.

4 In Darger's story, Blengin (short for Blengiglomeans) are supernatural creatures. She/he can be a composite of girl bodies with male genitalia, butterfly wings, horns, and serpent tails or animal bodies with serpent tails and multicolored wings. They are fierce protectors of children. For more on Blengins, see MacGregor, *In the Realms of the Unreal*, 346–411 and Bonesteel, *Henry Darger*, 170–193.

5 Lori Merish, "Cuteness and Commodity Aesthetics: Tom Thumb and Shirley Temple," in *Freakery: Cultural Spectacles of the Extraordinary Body*, edited by Rosemarie Garland Thomson (New York: New York University Press, 1996), 185–186.

6 Ibid, 188.

7 Several scholars reference and contextualize Konrad Lorenz's theory in their discussions on the aesthetic of cuteness. Some include: Joshua Paul Dale, Joyce Goggin, Julia Leyda, Anthony P. McIntyre, and Diane Negra, eds., *The Aesthetics and Affects of Cuteness* (New York: Routledge, 2017); Gary Genosko, "Natures and the Cultures of Cuteness," *Invisible Culture: An Electronic Journal for Visual Culture* (2005), accessed January 22, 2017, www.rochester.edu/in_visible_culture/Issue_9/genosko.html; Wan-Chuan Kao and Jen Boyle, eds., *The Retro-Futurism of Cuteness* (New York: Punctum Books, 2017).

8 Lorenz formulated these attributes in the 1940s and continued to refine them in following decades. See Konrad Lorenz, *The Foundations of Ethology* (New York: Springer-Verlag, 1981), 163–165.

9 Ibid, 154.

10 Gary Cross, *The Cute and the Cool: Wonderous Innocence and Modern American Children's Culture* (Oxford Scholarship Online, 2004), 34–35, DOI: 10.1093/acprof:oso/9780195156669.001.0001.

11 Ibid, 31.

12 Moon, *Henry Darger*, 92.

13 Trent, "Enigmatic Bachelors," 103.

14 Ibid.

15 Gavin Parkinson, "Henry Darger, Comics, and the Graphic Novel: Contexts and Appropriations," in *The Cambridge History of the Graphic Novel*, edited by Jan Baetens, Hugo Frey and Stephen E. Tabachnick (New York: Cambridge University Press, 2018), 145–149.

16 Ibid, 148.

17 Moon, *Henry Darger*, 84–85.

18 Mary Trent makes a brief note of the significance of Temple as a "New Kid" type as well as a few of Darger's resources pertaining to Temple. See Trent, "Enigmatic Bachelors," 101–102.

19 "Pee-Wee's Progress," *Time*, April 27, 1936, 36–44.

20 John Kasson, *The Little Girl Who Fought the Great Depression: Shirley Temple and 1930s America* (New York: W. W. Norton & Company, 2015), 87.
21 Ibid, 83.
22 Ibid, 78.
23 Henry Darger Papers (Box 76, Folder 4).
24 Ibid (Box 112).
25 Ibid (Box 109).
26 Daniel Thomas Cook, *The Commodification of Childhood: The Children's Clothing Industry and the Rise of the Child Consumer* (Durham, NC: Duke University Press, 2004), 92.
27 Daniel Harris, *Cute, Quaint, Hungry and Romantic: The Aesthetics of Consumerism* (New York: Basic Books, 2000), 91.
28 Quoted in MacGregor, *In the Realms of the Unreal*, 100.
29 Kasson, *The Little Girl Who Fought the Great Depression*, 128.
30 Claudia Nelson, *Little Strangers: Portrayals of Adoption and Foster Care in America, 1850–1929* (Bloomington: Indiana University Press, 2003), 66.
31 Ibid, 68.
32 Ibid, 121.
33 Kristen Hatch, *Shirley Temple and the Performance of Girlhood* (New Brunswick, NJ: Rutgers University Press, 2015), 2.
34 Merish, "Cuteness and Commodity Aesthetics," 195.
35 Hatch, *Shirley Temple and the Performance of Girlhood*, 5.
36 Ibid, 22.
37 Ibid, 10.
38 Merish, "Cuteness and Commodity Aesthetics," 197–200.
39 Ibid, 199–200.
40 Quoted in MacGregor, *In the Realms of the Unreal*, 286.
41 Jo-Ann Morgan, *Uncle Tom's Cabin as Visual Culture* (Columbia, MO: University of Missouri Press, 2007), 61–62; For more on the relationship between Temple and Little Eva as well as Temple's on-screen interactions with Robinson, see Hatch, *Shirley Temple and the Performance of Girlhood*, 83–105.
42 Darger, *In the Realms of the Unreal*, Volume I, 17.
43 Stowe, *Preface* of *Uncle Tom's Cabin*, 213.
44 For a cultural history of topsy-turvy dolls, see Robin Bernstein, *Racial Innocence: Performing American Childhood from Slavery to Civil Rights* (New York: New York University Press, 2011), 69–91 and Historical Folk Toys—Catalog Continuation Page: Topsy-Turvy Doll Kit, www.historicalfolktoys.com/catcont/4716.html.
45 Ricard Dyer, *White: Essays on Race and Culture* (Philadelphia, PA: Routledge, 1997), 1–2.
46 Kincaid coins this phrase in *Child Loving*.
47 Kincaid, *Erotic Innocence*, 120.
48 Ibid, 13.
49 See Bonesteel, *Henry Darger*, 10–11 and "Henry Darger's Search for the Grail," 261.
50 *The Leader*, Saturday, April 15, 1911, https://news.google.com/newspapers?id=f7RSAAAAIBAJ&pg=4594%2C5320618.
51 Description from *Chicago Daily News*, Friday, April 12, 1911, 2.
52 This association was first made by Michael Bonesteel.
53 Bonesteel, "Henry Darger's Search for the Grail," 264–265.

54 MacGregor, *In the Realms of the Unreal*, 498.
55 Trent, "'Many Stirring Scenes," 80.
56 Ibid, 83.
57 Moon, *Henry Darger*, 84–85.
58 Henry Darger Papers (Box 111).
59 Reverend Alphonse L. Memmesheimer, *My Child Lives: Consoling Thoughts for Bereaved Parents* (New York: Benziger Brothers, 1937), 46.
60 Ibid, 51.
61 Ibid, 53–54.
62 Darger, *In the Realms of the Unreal*, Volume VII, 500.
63 Galatians Galatians 5:22–23.
64 Quoted in MacGregor, *In the Realms of the Unreal*, 633.
65 Ibid, 5.
66 Harris, *Cute, Quaint, Hungry and Romantic*, 4.
67 Sianne Ngai, "The Cuteness of the Avant-Garde," *Critical Inquiry* 31:4 (Summer 2005): 816.
68 Harris, *Cute, Quaint, Hungry and Romantic*, 6.

Epilogue
Attentive Aesthetics

Multiple faces in *Untitled* (Figure 1.3) although mute, beg to tell a story. This story though, hides within the scene. In fact, *Untitled* resists narrative associations. Darger does not offer a caption. Nothing appears to be happening. *Untitled* dwells on a static display of little girls that crowd the foreground of an Edenic landscape. A horizon line, rising slightly above each of their heads, reiterates the flowing pitch of their collective heights. Just as the arrangement of girls swells into a soft mound of doubling cuties (one on top of the other), the horizon similarly ascends, encompassing girls within verdant space. Deciduous trees and palms, along with an occasional quaint cottage or stately home, dot the skyline. Below, varieties of posies, pansies, roses, tulips, cone flowers, and cacti propagate along the front edge of the scene. Giant flowers playfully commingle with the girl assortment, while other smaller floral versions tuck behind girls' ears or decorate their sundresses. Within this bountiful view, nature acts as a safe haven for the girls, enveloping them within its manicured beauty. Only the mounting, finger-like projections of distant clouds, far, far away, detract from the overall exuberant fecundity of this idyllic scene. Their capricious peaks indicate the sharp updrafts of heat and turbulent air, an approaching escalation of forces.

The uncertain space of the horizon holds this tension between a building unknown and a transitory peacefulness. It demarcates these two concurrent subtexts as well as the compositional planes of upper and lower registers. The horizontal axis organizes space, emitting a sweeping panoramic view. Darger capitalizes on this stretching format to achieve the orderly display of each figure, from head-to-toe. Even little girls standing behind the main group receive three-quarter length depiction as they appear to stand or sit upon the shoulders of those in front. While space extends into a deep perspective, such girl-on-girl juxtapositions counteract this effect and flatten out the composition.

In this scene, most of Darger's little girls stare back at us, acknowledging our presence and assuring us with their calm demeanor that our gaze is not intrusive, in fact, our gaze is consensual. Unifying facial direction toward the viewer (frontal, quarter-turned, or veering over the shoulder), intensifies their immobile bodies and penetrative gazes. Collectively, the girls look at the viewer; some, even with an unspecified focus, look through the viewer. This image becomes an encounter that acknowledges and implies the viewer's presence. Many of Darger's works after 1944 exhibit similar clusters of uniform girls that replicate and elevate above each other resulting in ample visibility of the face. This innovative, "girl wall" effect beckons the viewer's attention. The result is akin to what art historian Alois Riegl (1858–1905) referred to as a phenomenon of "external coherence" that occurs in seventeenth-century Dutch corporate portraiture.[1] His theory outlined the artistic role of the beholder and opened up art to socio-political interpretations beyond formal aesthetics. Like depicted figures in this Dutch tradition, Darger's girls in panoramic landscapes operate as autonomous individuals with a shared purpose—to construct a relationship with the viewer. Internally, within the painting these girls do not compositionally work together; their attentiveness to the viewer creates an implied sense of cohesion resulting not from formal composition but instead from this performative act.

Most girls stand side-by-side and gesture or slightly turn toward each other; some brandish cowboy boots or stir the contents of mixing bowls. Their stances reveal their commercial provenance from Wieboldt's and Sears clothing advertisements as well as their initial purpose to attract a consumer's attention as they pose in pretty frocks and sell goods. The aesthetic framework of paintings like *Untitled* operate in this very manner. A viewer is implied, and moreover, solicited to return multiple gazes in this reciprocal attention. This action acknowledges the viewer's function and gaze and thus, imaginatively connects to the viewer.

Beyond her embodiment of diminutive associations, gender fluidity, and cuteness, the little girl in Darger's art also functions as an aesthetic catalyst, a means to captivate image and viewer. So too, she acts as a surrogate for the viewer and locus of imaginary projection into vast distances and sprawling horizons. This little girl is part of Darger's own invitation, a visual appeal to an ever-present audience to exchange gazes with his protagonists or to follow their line of sight. Darger achieves the latter employing a panoramic view, imaginative projection, and again, little girls in *At Battle Near McHollister Run/At Wickey Sansinia* (Figure 3.4). A line of six Vivians in the foreground stand with their backs to the viewer. The girls' orientation is reminiscent of what the Dutch refer to as the figurative genre of *rugfiguur*, or back figure. Their bodily positioning renders them faceless, although they remain familiar through their girlish silhouettes. Each focuses on the distant horizon and, specifically, what Darger notes in the caption as a "coming storm." These girls invite the viewer to look deeply into the expanse and to anticipate an event yet to happen on the horizon. Consequently, the viewer is required to provide effort to navigate space and thus, this effort triggers an exchange between the threshold of the viewer's space and that of the protagonists. Girls in this scene remind us that we watch also. And, like the Vivians, we are witnesses before this story's endless sequence of events, a running narrative that rarely rests long enough to give in-depth consideration to the meaning of its violent and voluminous content.

Foregrounds of girls abut infinite horizons in Darger's panoramic schema as a means to fabricate not only a space (a world, a vision) big enough to hold a tremendous amount of detail, but also to build a sensate expanse capable of engaging a beholder. Like the engrossed attention of a girl army or a few Vivians gazing into the distance, the horizon and its panoramic reach unfold with ambiguity and aesthetic potential. Consider, for example, this passage from *In the Realms of the Unreal*:

> There was probably no one in the world who ever had the opportunity to gaze upon such a grand and magnificent scene as which was spread out before the vision from the summit (sic) of Gautamula ridge that bright early June day, 1913. Where ever you could look, from front, to rear, from left to right, the valleys stretched away in expanses of beautifully colored fields, and orchard and groves, and forests. And the very air was laden with the perfumes of all various spring flowers and of grasses, fresh pine and of fruits and with the incense of burning of dry dead leaves.
>
> Far above one could see large fleecy clouds floating athwart the blue expanse of sky, intercepting here and there the bright sunshine, and mottling the very landscape with alternate patches of light and shadow which chased each other from field to field, across hillock and stream. And through this fine setting of scenery in Northern Angelinia state passed an unusually magnificent panorama. If one looked down from the heights he could observe something long and gray following like the long windings of a snake, the meanderings of numerous roads, and thither to left and right up hill, and down dale, in sunshine and shadow, and this long line of gray, was tipped with shining steel, and threaded its way, a long serpent one reads of in fairy stories of old, here and there borne by a mounted orderly, a yellow gudion (sic) inscribed with the familiar devices belonging to the general headquarters, spoke the presence of a supreme chief general and his staff of general and other officers, followed by their retainers.[2]

Note the suggestive motion of a panorama "passing" through Northern Angelinia, as well as, the manner by which Darger describes the whole valley while weaving back and forth between the expanse and the detail, the general and the particular. Darger stuffs the scene full with palpable descriptions and movement: incense of burning leaves, perfume-laden air, fresh pine, fleecy clouds, mottled sunshine, shadows, snake-like winding, and shining steel. From this fluid narrative a troop of soldiers emerge, first appearing in the distance like a giant serpent and then slowly turning into marching lines of gray-garbed men, their steel weaponry glinting in the sunlight. Darger explores an indefatigable view, boundless and expansive, gradually offering a plethora of sights, textures, and smells. Here, Darger extends his storytelling device, the panorama, by utilizing an unfolding, continuous stream of descriptions and metamorphosing forms as a framework for imagining.

In word and image, Darger strove to provide enough detail and physical sensation to eliminate the distance between artist's vision and that of the spectator. This desire is specifically articulated in *In the Realms of the Unreal* introductory statements as Darger prepares the reader for a spectacular journey, he writes:

> But the reader, if he so wills, may keep his eye on all scenes that follow each other on and along the Aronburgs Run and its valley, for the final drama of the war will occur at or on the banks of the Aronburgs Run where the final ending of the hopes of successes for Glandelinia will ensue. . . . Let the reader follow battle after battle with the others, let him follow every event and adventure in the volume and then he can if he sets his mind and heart on it take on as if he himself was an actual participator.[3]

In his appeal to fabricate a palpable and affective connection to the war and the suffering of children, Darger asks us, "the reader," to be witnesses and participants in the telling of his story. Perhaps more than just a rhetorical device, this call invites a prospect of vicariously inhabiting events, even if remotely. He later compares his efforts to the aesthetic endeavors of "the poet, the painter and the artist," who "could not have accomplished anymore."[4] Elsewhere, he laments,

> . . . how can the weak pen and appalled, thrilled, and excited imaginations of the best and most learned of all writers and story tellers ever perform the task? Not even the very human heart can merely feel what language will never be able to express.[5]

While maintaining the extreme difficulty of fully describing his story in words, he heroically claims his best effort:

> I have written as far as I was able, in unusually long details to make the scenes more striking, but even then even I have not succeeded in

accomplishing what should have been done, as it is IMPOSSIBLE to describe them as they really are.[6]

Not only does Darger position himself as a war correspondent, struggling to faithfully describe events, but also from different politicized perspectives, even that of the victim. In the Introduction of Volume IV in *In the Realms of the Unreal*, he states:

> The author writes the scenes in this volume as if he often had experienced them himself, as if at one time he is on the side of the foe, at other on that of the Christians, then again he is with Penrod, and his friends, or with Violet, and her sisters, or with the Christian generals. Some times (sic) he writes as if he was actually one of the surviving victims of either flood, fire, or explosion disaster, or fights in battles from one side or another.[7]

As a result of metabolizing different forms of rhetoric, Darger also acquired (knowingly or unknowingly) an idiomatic use of witnessing as a device for conveying events beyond description. As literary historian Lea Wernick Fridman suggests, "Catastrophe, by its nature, exceeds the ability of the mind to grasp it."[8] Narratives of catastrophe, what she refers to as "historical horror," present the unique problem of "representing events that insist that they cannot be put into words even as they insist upon the need for transmission."[9] The testimony of a witness, whose telling equates with truth, offers another means of knowing when "traumatic fact cannot articulate itself credibly."[10]

These sentiments, coupled with the actuality that Darger executed visual pieces after writing the bulk of *In the Realms of the Unreal*, suggest that his imagery was not only a means to complement and complete his opus, but also to achieve something much greater. His admissions point toward the unique, provocative quality of the visual to shape awareness in viewers, even an awareness which was not fully translatable into words. Thus, he attempted to achieve visionary rather than visual potential capable of evoking highly subjective, experiential responses for himself and his imagined viewer. With evocative potentials, his visual work surpasses the merely illustrative, giving way to a less logical, more projective and imaginative mode of representation. Darger writes:

> As observed here, the desolation of the war in every incomprehensible way is everywhere stretched out, roaring into abuses of child slaves, increasing wicked wrongs, redoubling distresses, and bringing the attention of the world to the horrors of disasters that were never heard of in real experiences and history, thus bringing the sympathies of the world to the lowly child slaves, and Abbieannia's cause.[11]

Darger's choice of words: *increasing, stretching,* and *redoubling* accentuates his will to push beyond reality. To see all in Darger's world is to also see (endure) again (and again).[12] And, what we revisit are not just ordinary events, but profoundly extreme experiences—crimes, genocide, "horrors of disaster" and countervailing martyrdoms, miracles, and resurrections—acts and deeds that by their very heinous or revelatory nature insist that we move beyond passive seeing into an active and more emotive modality of witnessing. By surpassing reality, inflating the horrors to degrees of unbelievable proportions, his art enters into his imaginary realms of the unreal—the incomprehensible and "never heard of in real experiences and history." Here, a paradoxical problem emerges in Darger's art—describing the unknowable. As his imagery spirals off into an exponentially mounting panoramic vision of unreality, Darger clings to his impossible task of rendering the indescribable—the utter horror of relentless catastrophic experience that he cannot put into words. While this undertaking directly addresses his personalized, highly inventive project, his work also draws upon language and representational strategies employed in the telling of real historical warfare, tragedy, and crime including, but, not limited to, the social anxiety surrounding child orphans and the safety of children within his immediate cultural milieu.

Darger possessed a remarkable ability to repurpose images from popular culture and reinvent them for his own narrative. His Vivian, a little girl, triggers a wealth of responses, from the pleasure of recognizing her (a Sears Roebuck model or Morton Salt Girl) to spotting her recycled image in different scenarios, to the discomfort, even disgust, when later witnessing a Glandelinian strangling her. However, the act of tracing, literally and figuratively, left behind the residue of this little girl's origin. By showcasing and manipulating existing illustrations of girls from popular culture, Darger exposes their original subtext comprised of multivocal meanings springing from little, cute, and gendered associations. As the previous chapters attest, these meanings are complex, open-ended, and often in conflict with each other. The simple contours that Darger sketches to delineate the girl body contradict the complications inherent within her sweet image. Even though the Vivian Girl, as all of Darger's little girls, manifests in a comic book style—doll-like and fictitious—one cannot divorce one's feelings and fears from her culturally constructed texts. This girl, entangled within multiple narratives—colonized by Glandelinians, Darger's and the viewer's gaze—is a compelling interpretive site that is vulnerable to competing, even opposing claims. Moving between social and aesthetic conventions and codes, she emerges as a provocative or inert force. Her presence alone directs the tenor of Darger's art simply by her mutable, seductive, and attentive visage.

Notes

1 See Alois Riegl, *The Group Portraiture of Holland*, trans. Evelyn M. Kain and David Britt (Los Angeles: The Getty Research Institute for the History of Art and the Humanities, 1999) and Margaret Olin, *Forms of Representation in Alois Riegel's Theory of Art* (University Park: The Pennsylvania State University Press, 1992).

2 Darger, *In the Realms of the Unreal*, Book IV, Chapter 59, 914.

3 Ibid, Volume IV, unnumbered first page.

4 Ibid, Volume I, Chapter 3, Introduction, 1. As mentioned in footnote 57 of Chapter 1, this quote and that of footnote 11 in this Epilogue are appropriated revisions of writing from Harriet Beecher Stowe.

5 Ibid, Volume IV, 1407, Quoted by MacGregor, *In the Realms of the Unreal*, 99.

6 Ibid, Volume I, Chapter 3, Introduction, 1.

7 Ibid, Quoted in MacGregor, *In the Realms of the Unreal*, 184.

8 Lea Wernick Fridman, "History, Fantasy, Horror," in *Words and Witness: Narrative and Aesthetic Strategies in the Representation of the Holocaust* (Albany: State University of New York Press, 2000), 15.

9 Ibid, 6.

10 Ibid.

11 Darger, *In the Realms of the Unreal*, Volume III, Introduction, unnumbered page.

12 Darger often repeats figures within the same composition. Similar descriptions of battles, fires, etc. also recur with little variation throughout the story.

Selected Bibliography

Anderson, Brooke Davis, ed. *Darger: The Henry Darger Collection at the American Folk Art Museum.* New York: Harry N. Abrams, 2001.

Ariès, Philippe. *Centuries of Childhood: A Social History of Family Life*, translated by Robert Baldick. New York: Vintage Books, 1962.

Baum, L. Frank. *The Wonderful Wizard of Oz.* New York: HarperCollins Publishers, 1900 [1987].

Bernstein, Robin. *Racial Innocence: Performing American Childhood from Slavery to Civil Rights.* New York: New York University Press, 2011.

Biesenbach, Klaus, ed. *Henry Darger.* New York: Prestel Publishing, 2009.

Boehm, Lisa Krissoff. *Popular Culture and the Enduring Myth of Chicago, 1876–1968.* Philadelphia: Routledge, 2004.

Bonesteel, Michael. *Henry Darger: Art and Selected Writings.* New York: Rizzoli, 2000.

_____. "Henry Darger's Search for the Holy Grail in the Guise of a Celestial Child," in *Third Person: Authoring and Exploring Vast Narratives*, eds. Pat Harrigan and Noah Wardrip-Fruin. Cambridge, MA: MIT Press, 2009, 253–265.

Brown, Marilyn R., ed. *Picturing Children: Constructions of Childhood between Rousseau and Freud.* Burlington, VT: Ashgate Publishing, 2002.

Bynum, Caroline Walker. *Fragmentation and Redemption: Essays on Gender and the Human Body in Medieval Religion.* New York: Zone Books, 1991.

Cardinal, Roger. *Outsider Art.* New York: Praeger Publishers, 1972.

Castelli, Elizabeth. " 'I Will Make Mary Male': Pieties of the Body and Gender Transformation of Christian Women in Late Antiquity," in *Body Guards: The Cultural Politics of Gender Ambiguity*, eds. Julia Epstein and Kristina Straub. New York: Routledge Publishing, 1991, 29–49.

Cobb, L. Stephanie. *Dying to Be Men: Gender and Language in Early Christian Martyr Texts.* New York: Columbia University Press, 2008.

The Columbia Encyclopedia. "Daisy." 6th Edition. Columbia University Press. Accessed February 10, 2014. www.bartleby.com/65/ da/daisy.html.

Cook, Daniel Thomas. *The Commodification of Childhood: The Children's Clothing Industry and the Rise of the Child Consumer.* Durham: Duke University Press, 2004.

Cross, Gary. *The Cute and the Cool: Wonderous Innocence and Modern American Children's Culture.* Oxford Scholarship Online, 2004. DOI: 10.1093/acprof: oso/9780195156669.001.0001.

Dale, Joshua Paul, Joyce Goggin, Julia Leyda, Anthony P. McIntyre, and Diane Negra, eds. *The Aesthetics and Affects of Cuteness*. New York: Routledge Publishing, 2017.

Darger, Henry. *The History of My Life* (1967–70. Microfilm). New York: American Folk Art Museum Library and Archives, unpublished.

———. *The Story of the Vivian Girls, in What Is Known as the Realms of the Unreal, of the Glandeco-Angelinnian War Storm, Caused by the Child Slave Rebellion* (c. 1911–1939. Microfilm). New York: American Folk Art Museum Library and Archives, unpublished.

Donovan, Frank. *The Children of Charles Dickens*. London: Leslie Frewin, 1969.

Dubuffet, Jean. "Art Brut in Preference to the Cultural Arts." translated by Paul Foss and Allen S. Weiss, *Art & Text* 27 (1998): 31–33.

Dyer, Ricard. *White: Essays on Race and Culture*. Philadelphia: Routledge, 1997.

Fahs, Alice. "A Boys' and Girls' War," in *The Imagined Civil War: Popular Literature of the North & South, 1861–1865*. Chapel Hill: The University of North Carolina Press, 2001, 256–286.

Ferguson, George. *Signs and Symbols in Christian Art*. New York: Oxford University Press, 1955.

Fridman, Lea Wernick. *Words and Witness: Narrative and Aesthetic Strategies in the Representation of the Holocaust*. Albany: State University of New York Press, 2000.

Frohlich, Mary. *St. Thérèse of Lisieux: Essential Writings*. Maryknoll, NY: Orbis Books, 2003.

Furlong, Monica. *Thérèse of Lisieux*. London: Virago Press, 1987.

Gay & Lesbian Alliance against Defamation. "GLAAD Media Reference Guide." 10th Edition. October 2016. Accessed March 18, 2017. www.glaad.org/reference.

Genosko, Gary. "Natures and the Cultures of Cuteness." *Invisible Culture: An Electronic Journal for Visual Culture* (2005). Accessed January 22, 2017. www.rochester.edu/in_visible_culture/Issue_9/genosko.html.

"Girl Missing Gypsies Sought." *The Leader*. April 15, 1911. https://news.google.com/newspapers?id=f7RSAAAAIBAJ&pg=4594%2C532.

Greeley, Andrew. *The Catholic Imagination*. Berkeley: University of California Press, 2000.

Green, Eli R. and Luca Maurer. *The Teaching Transgender Toolkit: A Facilitator's Guide to Increasing Knowledge, Decreasing Prejudice & Building Skills*. Ithaca, NY: Planned Parenthood of the Southern Finger Lakes: Out for Health, 2015. Accessed March 18, 2017. www.teachingtransgender.org.

Grossman, James R., ed. *The Encyclopedia of Chicago*. Chicago: The University of Chicago Press, 2004.

Harris, Daniel. *Cute, Quaint, Hungry and Romantic: The Aesthetics of Consumerism*. New York: Basic Books, 2000.

Hatch, Kristen. *Shirley Temple and the Performance of Girlhood*. New Brunswick, NJ: Rutgers University Press, 2015.

Henry Darger Papers. New York: American Folk Art Museum Library and Archives.

Henry Darger Room Collection and Archives. Chicago: Intuit, The Center for Intuitive and Outsider Art.

Higonnet, Anne. *Pictures of Innocence: The History and Crisis of Ideal Childhood*. London: Thames and Hudson, 1988.

"Historical Folk Toys—Catalog Continuation Page: Topsy-Turvy Doll Kit." Accessed June 15, 2020. www.historicalfolktoys.com/catcont/4716.html.

Howie, Elizabeth. "Indulgence and Refusal: Cuteness, Asceticism, and the Aestheticization of Desire," in *The Retro-Futurism of Cuteness*, eds. Jen Boyle and Wan-Chuan Kao. New York: Punctum Books, 2017, 53–63.

In the Realms of the Unreal: The Mystery of Henry Darger, Directed by Jessica Yu. Los Angeles: Diorama Films, 2004.

Kasson, John. *The Little Girl Who Fought the Great Depression: Shirley Temple and 1930s America*. New York: W. W. Norton & Company, 2015.

Kincaid, James R. *Child-Loving: The Erotic Child and Victorian Culture*. London: Routledge, 1994.

_____. *Erotic Innocence: The Culture of Child Molesting*. Durham: Duke University Press, 1998.

Laing, Olivia. "The Realms of the Unreal," in *The Lonely City: Adventures in the Art of Being Alone*. New York: Picador, 2016, 135–178.

Laqueur, Thomas. *Making Sex; Body and Gender for the Greeks to Freud*. Cambridge, MA: Harvard University Press, 1992.

Latin Dictionary and Grammar Aid. "Vivam" by Cawley, Kevin. Accessed January 10, 2014. http://catholic.archives.nd.edu/latgramm.htm.

Lorenz, Konrad. *The Foundations of Ethology*. New York: Springer-Verlag, 1981.

Low, Juliette Gordon. "How Girls Can Help Their Country." *Open Collections Program, Harvard University Libraries*. Accessed June 12, 2006. http://pds.harvard.edu:8080/pdx/servlet/pds?

MacGregor, John M. *Henry Darger: In the Realms of the Unreal*. New York: Delano Greenidge, 2002.

_____. "Thoughts on the Question: Why Darger?" *The Outsider* 2:2 (Winter 1998): 12–16.

Memmesheimer, Reverend Alphonse L. *My Child Lives: Consoling Thoughts for Bereaved Parents*. New York: Benziger Brothers, 1937.

Merish, Lori. "Cuteness and Commodity Aesthetics: Tom Thumb and Shirley Temple," in *Freakery: Cultural Spectacles of the Extraordinary Body*, ed. Rosemarie Garland Thomson. New York: New York University Press, 1996, 185–206.

Metcalf, Eugene W. Jr. "From Domination to Desire: Insiders and Outsider Art," in *The Artist Outsider: Creativity and the Boundaries of Culture*, eds. Eugene W. Metcalf Jr. and Michael D. Hall. Washington, DC: Smithsonian Institution Press, 1994, 212–227.

Miles, Margaret. *Carnal Knowing: Female Nakedness and Religious Meaning in the Christian West*. Boston: Beacon Press, 1989.

Moon, Michael. *Darger's Resources*. Durham: Duke University Press, 2012.

Morgan, Jo-Ann. *Uncle Tom's Cabin as Visual Culture*. Columbia, MO: University of Missouri Press, 2007.

Nelson, Claudia. *Little Strangers: Portrayals of Adoption and Foster Care in America, 1850–1929*. Bloomington: Indiana University Press, 2003.

Ngai, Sianne. "The Cuteness of the Avant-Garde." *Critical Inquiry* 31:4 (Summer 2005): 811–827.

Olin, Margaret. *Forms of Representation in Alois Riegel's Theory of Art*. University Park: The Pennsylvania State University Press, 1992.

Oxford English Dictionary. "Cute." Accessed March 10, 2020. https://www-oed-com.proxy177.nclive.org/view/Entry/46355?rskey=GtWQvQ&result=3&isAdvanced=false#eid.

Parkinson, Gavin. "Henry Darger, Comics, and the Graphic Novel: Contexts and Appropriations," in *The Cambridge History of the Graphic Novel*, eds. Jan Baetens, Hugo Frey, and Stephen E. Tabachnick. New York: Cambridge University Press, 2018, 139–154.

"Pee-Wee's Progress." *Time* XXVII (1936): 36–44.

Perkins, Judith. *The Suffering Self: Pain and Narrative Representation in the Early Christian Era*. New York: Routledge, 1995.

Powers, Ann Bleigh Powers. "The Joan of Arc Vogue in America, 1894–1929." *American Society for the Legion of Honor* 49:3 (1978): 177–192.

Remarque, Erich Maria. *All Quiet on the Western Front*, translated by A. W. Wheen. Boston: Little, Brown & Company, 1986 [1929].

Rhodes, Colin. *Outsider Art: Spontaneous Alternatives*. New York: Thames and Hudson, 2000.

Riegl, Alois. *The Group Portraiture of Holland*, translated by Evelyn M. Kain and David Britt. Los Angeles: The Getty Research Institute for the History of Art and the Humanities, 1999.

Rundquist, Leisa. "Little Ways: Girlhood According to Henry Darger." *Southeastern College Art Conference Review* XV:4 (2009): 434–447.

———. "Vivam! The Divine Intersexuality of Henry Darger's Vivian Girl." *Elsewhere: The International Journal of Self-Taught and Outsider Art* 2 (May 2014): 24–42.

Sackville-West, Vita. *The Eagle and the Dove*. London: Michael Joseph, 1943.

Saward, John. *The Way of the Lamb: The Spirit of Childhood and the End of the Age*. San Francisco: Ignatius Press, 1999.

Seaton, Beverly. *The Language of Flowers: A History*. Charlottesville: University Press of Virginia, 1995.

Speake, Jennifer. *The Dent Dictionary of Symbols in Christian Art*. London: J.M. Dent, 1994.

Stead, William T. *If Christ Came to Chicago!* Chicago: Laird & Lee, 1894.

Streete, Gail P. C. "Tough Mothers and Female Contenders," in *Redeemed Bodies: Women Martyrs in Early Christianity*. Louisville, KY: Westminster John Knox Press, 2009, 49–72.

Stowe, Harriet Beecher. *Uncle Tom's Cabin, or Life among the Lowly*. New York: Bantam Books, 1981 [1851–1852].

Stewart, Susan. *On Longing: Narratives of the Miniature, the Gigantic, the Souvenir, the Collection*. Durham: Duke University Press, 1993.

Trent, Mary. "Enigmatic Bachelors: Masculinity, Girlhood, and Vision in the Art of Joseph Cornell and Henry Darger." PhD diss., University of California, Irvine, 2010.

———. "Many Stirring Scenes: Henry Darger's Reworking of American Visual Culture." *American Art* 26:1 (2012): 75–101.

Warner, Marina. *Alone of All Her Sex: The Myth and the Cult of the Virgin Mary*. New York: Vintage Books, 1983.

_____. *Fantastic Metamorphosis: Other Worlds: Ways of Telling the Self*. New York: Oxford University Press, 2002.

_____. *Joan of Arc: The Image of Female Heroism*. Berkeley: University of California Press, 1999.

_____. "Memories of the Martyrs: Reflections from a Catholic Girlhood," in *Perpetua's Passions: Multidisciplinary Approaches to the Passio Perpetuae et Felicitatis*, eds. Jan N. Bremmer and Marco Formisano. New York: Oxford University Press, 2012, 348–365.

Weitbrecht, Julia. "Maternity and Sainthood in the Medieval Perpetua Legend," in *Perpetua's Passions: Multidisciplinary Approaches to the Passio Perpetuae*, eds. Jan N. Bremmer and Marco Formisano. New York: Oxford University Press, 2012, 150–166.

What Is the Definition of Intersex? Sudbury, MA: InterACT, Advocates for Intersex Youth. Accessed June 18, 2020. www.interactadvocates.org/faq/#definition.

Williams, Craig. "Perpetua's Gender: A Latinist Reads the *Passio Perpetuae et Felicitas*," in *Perpetua's Passions: Multidisciplinary Approaches to the Passio Perpetuae*, eds. Jan N. Bremmer and Marco Formisano. New York: Oxford University Press, 2012, 54–77.

Wilson, Colin. *The Outsider*. New York: Penguin Putnam, 1982 [1967 & 1956].

Winstead, Karen. *Virgin Martyrs: Legends of Sainthood in Late Medieval England*. Ithaca: Cornell University Press, 1997.

Wogan-Browne, Jocelyn. "Chaste Bodies: Frames and Experiences," in *Framing Medieval Bodies*, eds. Sarah Kay and Miri Rubin. Manchester: Manchester University Press, 1994.

Wojcik, Daniel. *Outsider Art: Visionary Worlds and Trauma*. Jackson, MS: University Press of Mississippi, 2016.

Zelizer, Viviana A. *Pricing the Priceless Child: The Changing Social Value of Children*. New York: Basic Books, 1985.

Index

Note: Page numbers in *italics* indicate a figure on the corresponding page.

For Product Safety Concerns and Information please contact our EU
representative GPSR@taylorandfrancis.com
Taylor & Francis Verlag GmbH, Kaufingerstraße 24, 80331 München, Germany